U·X·L newsmakers

U·X·L newsmakers

volume **4** four

Rodr–Z

Judy Galens,
Kelle S. Sisung

Carol Brennan, *Contributing Writer*

Jennifer York Stock, *Project Editor*

U·X·L
*An imprint of Thomson Gale,
a part of The Thomson Corporation*

THOMSON
—★—
GALE

Detroit • New York • San Francisco • San Diego • New Haven, Conn. • Waterville, Maine • London • Munich

U•X•L Newsmakers

Judy Galens, Kelle S. Sisung, and Carol Brennan

Project Editor
Jennifer York Stock

Editorial
Michael D. Lesniak, Allison McNeill

Rights Acquisition and Management
Peggie Ashlevitz, Edna Hedblad, Sue Rudolph

Imaging and Multimedia
Lezlie Light, Mike Logusz, Denay Wilding

Product Design
Kate Scheible

Composition
Evi Seoud

Manufacturing
Rita Wimberly

LIBRARY OF CONGRESS CATALOGING-IN-PUBLICATION DATA

Galens, Judy, 1968-

UXL newsmakers / Judy Galens and Kelle S. Sisung ; Allison McNeill, project editor.

p. cm.

Includes bibliographical references and index.

ISBN 0-7876-9189-5 (set) — ISBN 0-7876-9190-9 (v. 1)—ISBN 0-7876-9191-7 (v. 2)—ISBN 0-7876-9194-1 (v. 3)—ISBN 0-7876-9195-X (v. 4)

1. Biography—20th century—Dictionaries, Juvenile. 2. Biography—21st century—Dictionaries, Juvenile. 3. Celebrities—Biography—Dictionaries, Juvenile. I. Sisung, Kelle S. II. McNeill, Allison. III. Title.

CT120.G26 2004
920'.009'051—dc22

2004009426

Printed in the United States of America
10 9 8 7 6 5 4 3 2 1

contents

 contents

 volume **2** two

volume **③** three

 contents

volume **4** four

Italic type *indicates volume number.*

Entertainment

Government

Music

Science

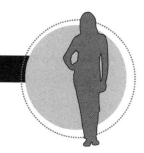

Social Issues

Sports

Writing

U•*X*•*L Newsmakers* is the place to turn for information on personalities active on the current scene. Containing one hundred biographies, *U*•*X*•*L Newsmakers* covers contemporary figures who are making headlines in a variety of fields, including entertainment, government, literature, music, pop culture, science, and sports. Subjects include international figures, as well as people of diverse ethnic backgrounds.

Format

Biographies are arranged alphabetically across four volumes. Each entry opens with the individual's birth date, place of birth, and field of endeavor. Entries provide readers with information on the early life, influences, and career of the individual or group being profiled. Most entries feature one or more photographs of the subject, and all entries provide a list of sources for further reading about the individual or group. Readers may also locate entries by using the Field of Endeavor table of contents listed in the front of each volume, which lists biographees by vocation.

Features

• A Field of Endeavor table of contents, found at the front of each volume, allows readers to access the biographees by the category for which they are best known. Categories include: Art/Design, Business, Entertainment, Government, Music, Science, Social Issues, Sports, and Writing. When applicable, subjects are listed under more than one category for even greater access.

• Sidebars include information relating to the biographee's career and activities (for example, writings, awards, life milestones), brief biographies of related individuals, and explanations of movements, groups, and more, connected with the person.

• Quotes from and about the biographee offer insight into their lives and personal philosophies.

• More than 180 black-and-white photographs are featured across the volumes.

- Sources for further reading, including books, magazine articles, and Web sites, are provided at the end of each entry.

- A general index, found at the back of each volume, quickly points readers to the people and subjects discussed in *U•X•L Newsmakers*.

Comments and Suggestions

The individuals chosen for these volumes were drawn from all walks of life and from across a variety of professions. Many names came directly from the headlines of the day, while others were selected with the interests of students in mind. By no means is the list exhaustive. We welcome your suggestions for subjects to be profiled in future volumes of *U•X•L Newsmakers* as well as comments on this work itself. Please write: Editor, *U•X•L Newsmakers,* U•X•L, 27500 Drake Road, Farmington Hills, Michigan 48331-3535; call toll-free: 1-800-877-4253; or send an e-mail via www.gale.com.

U·X·L newsmakers 1

Alex Rodríguez

July 27, 1975 • *New York, New York*

Baseball player

Baseball fans say that Alex Rodríguez may just break a number of career records in the game. Before he joined the New York Yankees in 2004 he had already achieved the famous "40-40" number: forty home runs and forty stolen bases in one season. He was the first infielder in the history of the game to achieve it. But "A-Rod," as fans call him, also broke another significant record off the baseball diamond. In 2000 the Texas Rangers signed him to a record $252 million, ten-year contract. It made him the highest paid athlete in American sports history.

Father left the family

The future baseball great was born Alexander Emmanuel Rodríguez in New York City in 1975, and had two older siblings. His father, Victor, had been a baseball player back in the Dominican Republic, but was running a shoe store in Manhattan by the time the third Rodríguez child was born. In 1979, when Rodríguez was four years old, Victor retired and took his family to the Dominican Republic. The family lived there for three years, and moved back to the United States when Rodríguez was seven. They settled in Miami, Florida, but Victor, who had taught his son the basics of baseball, left the family a few years later.

With the family finances tight, Rodríguez's mother, Lourdes, had to work two jobs. By day she was a secretary at the local immigration office. At night she waited tables in a restaurant. "When Mom got home, I'd always count her tip money to see how good she did," Rodríguez recalled in an interview with *People* writer Alex Tresniowski. "She taught me the meaning of hard work and commitment."

> **"I don't get caught up in the hype. I'd play even if I had to pay someone to let me play."**

Lourdes also encouraged her son's love of baseball. He played for the local Boys & Girls Clubs of Miami teams, where a coach, Eddie Rodríguez (no relation to the family), pushed him to excel and came to serve as a father-figure. At Miami's Westminster Christian High School, Rodríguez emerged as an outstanding athlete in both football and baseball. Scouts for Major League Baseball (MLB) teams came to see him play, and he became the top pick in the June draft of 1993.

Made it through tough rookie year

Rodríguez was signed by the Seattle Mariners, but he and his mother had also hired a hard-nosed agent, Scott Boras, to hammer out the details of his contract. The negotiations lasted all summer. He was all set to put his backup plan in motion and enter the University of Miami, but just hours before his first class was about to start, the Mariners agreed to a $1.3 million, three-year contract.

During his first season Rodríguez played for all the teams in the Seattle organization. He first played in Appleton, Wisconsin, and then

A-Rod's Dad

Alex Rodríguez was nine years old when his father, Victor, left the family. The former Dominican Republic ball player and shoe store owner reportedly wanted to move back to New York City, while Rodríguez's mother, Lourdes, wanted to stay in Miami. The boy was not told at first about the split, although his older brother and sister knew the truth. "I kept thinking my father would come back, but he never did," Rodríguez recalled in an interview with *Sports Illustrated* writer Gerry Callahan.

Rodríguez inherited his love of baseball from his father. But because his mother worked two jobs to support the family, it was hard for her to come to watch his youth league games. Rodríguez recalled the sadness he felt when he saw his teammates' fathers cheer their sons. "After a while, I lied to myself," Rodríguez admitted in a 1998 *Seattle Times* interview. "I tried to tell myself that it didn't matter, that I didn't care. But times I was alone, I often cried. Where was my father?"

Rodríguez emerged as a talented high school player and was drafted by the Seattle Mariners. The news of the draft was chronicled in the newspapers,

and Rodríguez's father finally contacted him that same week. "I didn't even know where he was calling from," Rodríguez told the *Seattle Times*. "I didn't know what to think. It was nice, but it didn't make much impression on me, not after all that time." The next year, when Rodríguez had been sent down to the Dominican Republic to play in its winter baseball league, his father showed up one day at batting practice. "When this man told me who he was, I almost broke down," Rodríguez told the *Seattle Times*. They talked and made plans to meet the next day, but Rodríguez cancelled their lunch appointment.

But Victor Rodríguez also read the *Seattle Times* article, and was saddened. The superstar athlete also felt a little bit of remorse, and arranged to have a satellite television dish delivered to his estranged father's house so that he could watch the Mariners' games. They met the following winter, and had another reunion that took place on Father's Day of 2000. "I wish I could tell you I had planned it that way," Rodríguez told the *Seattle Times* afterward, about the symbolic holiday meeting. "But I only thought that it was time, that I was ready and that I wanted to see my dad."

went on to a Class AA team in Jacksonville, Florida. Then the Mariners' coach, Lou Piniella (1943–), decided to bring him in for his first Major League game. Rodríguez was just eighteen years old when he played in his first MLB game at Fenway Park in Boston on July 8, 1994. He was the youngest player in ten years to make his Major League debut.

After a few more Mariners' games, Rodríguez was sent to play winter baseball in the Dominican Republic for extra practice. He did poorly in that 1994-95 season, batting just .179, and went up against many young and talented players from around the world. "It was the toughest experience of my life," he told *Sports Illustrated*'s Gerry

Callahan. "I just got my tail kicked and learned how hard this game can be. It was brutal, but I recommend it to every young player."

Rodríguez played again with the Mariners during the 1995 season. He was thrilled when they beat the New York Yankees for the American League East title, though he made few post-season appearances on the field. He finished the year with a batting average of .232. But in 1996 Rodríguez began to shine as the Mariners' shortstop in his first full season in the majors. He also was the season base leader in the League that year, at 379, breaking a record that had held since 1955. In the Most Valuable Player (MVP) contest, one of the League's most coveted awards, he lost out by just three votes to Juan González (1969–).

Dubbed "A-Rod"

However, the sports journalists who cast their ballots for the MVP award also began to describe Rodríguez as one of the most promising new athletes in the game. *Sports Illustrated* magazine featured him on the cover in July of 1996, and in the accompanying article Gerry Callahan wrote that the six-foot, three-inch Rodríguez was "195 pounds of pure skill and grace, an immensely gifted shortstop who routinely leaves baseball people drooling over their clipboards. He can run, hit, hit for power and make all the plays in the field." *Sporting News* named him Player of the Year after the regular season finished. Shortstop Ernie Banks (1931–), who had set the 379 bases record back in 1955, was enthusiastic about Rodríguez's future. "Alex Rodriguez is going to do things I never came close to doing," Banks told *Sporting News* writer Rob Rains. "I don't want to put pressure on him, but he's going to set a new standard for shortstops."

With such numbers, Rodríguez—now known among baseball fans by his nickname "A-Rod"—and his agent had little trouble negotiating a new contract with the Mariners, one that gave the player $10.6 million over the next four years. But Rodríguez hit a rough patch the next year, with just a .300 batting average and only 23 home runs for the season, although the Mariners finished the 1997 season once again in first place in the American League West. He had a better year in 1998: he became only the third player in MLB history to achieve the 40-40 number, with 42 home runs and 46 stolen bases. Only Jose Canseco (1964–) and Barry Bonds (1964–) had attained

40-40 before him, and Rodríguez was also the first infielder in base-ball history to hit that mark.

Rodríguez's second contract expired at the end of the 2000 season and he became a free agent, which left him free to sign his own deal with any other team. There was talk that he might join the New York Mets, but the negotiations stalled. He was on a December vacation in Las Vegas with some friends when Boras, his agent, phoned him to tell him the news that made headlines soon afterward: Boras had negotiated a contract for Rodríguez with the Texas Rangers that gave him $252 million over ten years. It was a baseball and professional sports record that amounted to about $170,270 a game for Rodríguez.

The Rangers' new hope

But Rodríguez was joining a troubled team that usually finished in last place in their league's division, the American League West. The Arlington-based team was owned by a Dallas investor named Tom Hicks. In 1998 Hicks had paid $250 million for the Rangers. He bought the team from a group of investors that included Texas Gover-nor George W. Bush (1946–). Rodríguez's record salary deal was announced in December of 2000, just as Bush was about to leave the governor's office for the White House. The newest Texas Ranger was the talk of Texas, and even the president-elect weighed in on the mat-ter. "When you pay more for your shortstop than you paid for your team, that ought to be a warning sign that your labor costs are out of control," Bush told *Texas Monthly*'s Paul Burka.

Rodríguez was deemed the man to lead the team to victory in 2001. The Rangers, it was said, were buying not only Rodríguez's impressive athletic talents, but also some of the A-Rod star power that would bring more fans to games at the Rangers' ballpark in Arlington. Others criticized him for setting an entirely new record in baseball as the highest paid player in a sport that already signed astronomical paychecks. At the Rangers' first game at Safeco Field, his former Seattle fans jeered him. Some even held up signs with nasty com-ments and a new nickname: "Pay-Rod."

The Rangers did poorly, despite Rodríguez's impressive statis-tics. The team remained in fourth place in the American League West

Alex Rodriguez fields a ball during practice with the New York Yankees. AP/Wide World Photos. Reproduced by permission.

standings, finishing 73-89 in 2001 and 72-90 in 2002. Meanwhile Rodríguez continued to set home run records. He reached number forty-eight in September of 2001, a new League record for home runs hit by shortstops. On April 30, 2002, he became the second youngest player in baseball history to hit 250 career home runs.

Back in hometown

But Rodríguez's talents could not save a struggling team, and attendance at the ballpark plummeted during 2003. With ticket sales down,

Hicks was forced to trade Rodríguez, whom he could no longer afford to keep. There was talk that Rodríguez might sign with the Boston Red Sox, but instead the Rangers traded him to the legendary New York Yankees in February of 2004. Since his friend, Derek Jeter (1974–), was already the shortstop for the New York team, Rodríguez was hired to play third base at the famous Yankee Stadium in the Bronx.

New York's large Dominican-American community was over-joyed by the news. Rodríguez had spent the first four years of his life in Washington Heights, the section of Manhattan where a large num-ber of Dominican Americans live, and had cousins who still lived in the area. He was also happy to be playing for a powerhouse team. The Yankees' owner was a fierce, vastly wealthy business mogul named George Steinbrenner (1930–), and the team was known as the richest in baseball. Steinbrenner regularly sought to sign the top players in the game, and it showed. Since 1996 the Yankees had made it to six World Series playoffs and won four of those contests.

Rodríguez is married to Cynthia, a school teacher, and has said that he still hopes to earn his college degree and perhaps even a gradu-ate business degree some day. One of his dreams is to own a small Italian restaurant. *Fast Company* writer Alan Schwarz asked Rodríguez, the son of immigrants from one of the poorest countries in the Western Hemisphere, if he thinks he is "living the American dream." The highest paid athlete in professional sports said no, not yet. "To me," he replied, "the American dream is all about having a family, raising kids, spending time with them at the end of the day, and sending them to college."

For More Information

Periodicals

Burka, Paul. "Spare the A-Rod." *Texas Monthly* (February 2001): p. 7.

Callahan, Gerry. "The Fairest of Them All." *Sports Illustrated* (July 8, 1996): p. 38.

"For Alex, Move to New York Has Taste of Home." *New York Daily News* (February 16, 2004). This article can also be found online at http://www.nydailynews.com.

Knisley, Michael. "All A-Rod All the Time." *Sporting News* (June 28, 1999): p. 12.

"Missing Dad in the 13 Years Since His Father Left, Alex Rodriguez Has Found Fortune and Fame in Seattle, But Has Been Unable to Reconcile with the Man Who Vanished. (Sports.)" *Seattle Times* (March 22, 1998): p. D1.

Rains, Rob. "A New Standard. (Player of the Year Winner Alex Rodriguez.)" *Sporting News* (October 14, 1996): p. 19.

Ribowsky, Mark. "The Ancient Mariner?" *Sport* (July 2000): p. 32.

"Rodriguez, Estranged Father Take Steps to Restore Bond." *Seattle Times* (June 23, 2000): p. D8.

Schwarz, Alan. "60 Seconds with Alex Rodriguez." *Fast Company* (September 2003): p. 44.

Stein, Joel. "Lord of the Swings: It's Hard Not to Like A-Rod, Baseball's Best, Best-Paid and Most Diplomatic Player. Except That He's a Yankee." *Time* (April 5, 2004): p. 68.

Tresniowski, Alex. "Golden Guy: The Big Bucks Stop Here, in the Sure Hands of Texas Shortstop Alex Rodriguez." *People* (April 16, 2001): p. 83.

Verducci, Tom. "Stumbling Start: Already Paying Dividends for the Rangers off the Field, Alex Rodriguez Tripped All over Himself During His Debut with Texas." *Sports Illustrated* (April 9, 2001): p. 56.

Verducci, Tom. "The Lone Ranger: Everyone Knows Alex Rodriguez Is Baseball's Highest-Paid Player, but Unless You're a Die-Hard Fan of Last-Place Texas, You Might Not Realize He's the Best Player in the Game." *Sports Illustrated* (September 9, 2002): p. 34.

Web Sites

"Timeline: Alex Rodriguez." *SI.com: Sports Illustrated.* http://sports illustrated.cnn.com/baseball/mlb/features/Rodriguez/timeline/ (accessed on June 12, 2004).

Burt Rutan

June 17, 1943 • Portland, Oregon

Aerospace engineer

Burt Rutan designed the first privately financed spacecraft to carry an ordinary citizen into space. On a June morning in 2004, Rutan's innovative *SpaceShipOne* rose from the Mojave Desert in California, flown by test pilot Mike Melvill (c. 1942–), climbed through the clouds, and entered space. It was an important date in the history of aviation, and Rutan hoped it would be the start of a new era of adventure travel—that of space tourism.

Built model airplanes

Rutan and his brother, Richard (1938–), a former U.S. Air Force combat pilot, have been aviation pioneers for nearly all of their adult lives. Born Elbert L. Rutan on June 17, 1943, in Portland, Oregon, Rutan grew up in Dinuba, a town in California's Central Valley area. The Rutans' father, a dentist, had a pilot's license and owned a small plane. Both Rutan and his brother were fascinated by air travel as youngsters. Dick was five years older than Burt and sometimes refused to let him play with his collection of model aircraft. In response, Burt began building his own.

The Rutan brothers entered model plane contests in the area, and Burt soon became known as a clever designer. One race involved mimicking the fighter planes that land on aircraft carriers. "Burt built a plane that looked like a contemporary Navy fighter," Dick recalled in an interview for *Smithsonian* with Edwards Park. "Then he worked out how to do a power stall with it. The thing would almost hover over the deck, tail down, engine full on, until he dropped it at exactly the right spot and engaged the arresting gear. He always won."

"I don't care about taking the risk that something won't succeed. That's the big difference between me and the engineers who work in aerospace. Or the managers of the engineers who work in aerospace. They're absolutely frightened of failure."

Before he obtained his own driver's license, Rutan often had his mother take him out on the back roads near their home with one of his new model airplane designs. He instructed her to drive fast, so that he could test the aerodynamics of his latest model plane by holding the plane out the window. Aerodynamics is a scientific term that refers to the study of the effect of air and other gases on objects in motion. When he was in college at California State Polytechnic University, Rutan even built his own small wind tunnel, a device that scientists use to conduct tests in aerodynamics. He installed it atop his Dodge Dart station wagon to help him refine his designs. These experiments led him to build his first full-size plane, which he called the VariViggen.

Breaking Earth's Bounds

September 9, 1908: U.S. Army Lieutenant Frank P. Lahm becomes the first passenger to travel in an airplane. Lahm rides along on a six-minute flight with airplane co-inventor Wilbur Wright at Fort Meyer, Virginia.

March 16, 1926: American rocket pioneer Robert Goddard makes first successful launch of a liquid-fueled rocket, in Auburn, Massachusetts.

October 14, 1947: American pilot Chuck Yeager is recorded as the first human to break the sound barrier of 660 miles per hour in a Bell SX-1 rocket plane.

September 7, 1956: U.S. test pilot Iven C. Kincheloe becomes first person to reach space after being launched from a B-50 U.S. Air Force plane.

Kincheloe and his smaller Bell X-2 rocket plane peaked at 126,500 feet above Earth and landed safely. He died in another test flight two years later.

March 30, 1961: American test pilot Joe Walker reaches an altitude of 169,600 feet in an X-15 rocket plane.

April 12, 1961: Yuri Gagarin of the Soviet Union becomes the first human to orbit Earth.

April 12, 1981: The *Columbia* space shuttle becomes the first winged vehicle in orbit, and also makes the first runway landing of a spacecraft in history.

April 12, 2001: American Dennis Tito buys a seat on the Russian *Soyuz* craft and becomes the first tourist in space.

Founded own company

In 1965 Rutan graduated third in his class at Cal State Polytechnic with an aeronautical engineering degree. He went to work as a civilian flight test project engineer at Edwards Air Force Base, the U.S. military facility near Mojave, California, which is the site of nearly all of the aviation records set in the latter half of the twentieth century. During his seven years there, Rutan helped fixed a troubling flaw in the F-4 fighter jet. The U.S. military had spent a small fortune to build it, but the F-4 sometimes went into flat spins and crashed. Rutan came up with a way to give it better in-flight stability and devised a recovery system for the times it went into a spin.

Rutan left Edwards in 1972 to become the director of flight testing for the Bede Aircraft Company in Newton, Kansas. He also continued to work on his own plane designs. But Rutan felt that his innovative ideas would never reach others if he tried to work with traditional airplane manufacturing companies. In June of 1974 he founded the Rutan Aircraft Factory (known as RAF) in Mojave. It produced and sold designs for the VariViggen and other light aircraft that could be built at home by do-it-yourself enthusiasts. RAF quickly became a leader in aviation design, and Rutan a hero among the engineers and pilots who liked to build their own small planes. His VariEze aircraft, for example, was made out of lightweight composite material and had a small extra wing in the nose called a canard. If a plane experienced a problem in mid-flight, the canard lost lift first, not the main wing. This allowed the pilot to stabilize the plane.

For many years Rutan tested his planes himself, or had his brother pilot them. They showed off the newest RAF models at annual Experimental Aircraft Association shows. But Rutan had some near-misses, and quit testing planes after a friend of his died in 1978. His brother, however, was eager to take on one of the final challenges left in aviation: a non-stop, around-the-world flight. Over dinner one evening in 1981, Rutan sketched on a napkin his idea for a new kind of plane. It would have space for enough fuel to make the 24,986-mile trip without stopping to fill the tank. Previously, the distance record was held by a U.S. B-52 bomber, which flew from Okinawa, Japan, to Madrid, Spain, in 1962, without refueling or stopping. U.S. Air Force planes had made similar trips in the 1940s and 1950s, but were refueled in mid-air.

Nine-day flight

The plane that Rutan designed, the *Voyager I,* made its historic flight in December of 1986. It carried 7,011 pounds of fuel in tanks that looked similar to a pair of outriggers on a canoe. Its cabin, with room for Rutan's brother and his co-pilot, Jeana Yeager (1952–), was the size of a small closet. They had to be in a reclining position to fly the plane, which was as loud as a lawn mower. The flight took nine days.

During the entire time, Rutan kept in contact with his brother and Yeager from a command center at Edwards Air Force Base. He talked them through more than one bout of bad weather, including a typhoon over the Pacific Ocean. "Our own data said that the Voyager flight was probably not going to happen," Rutan told Andy Meisler of the *New York Times* several years later. "We had seven major failures in the 340 hours the plane had flown, and we were planning a 225-hour single flight, almost all over oceans. As far as the pilots' fatigue and their ability to stand up under even moderate levels of turbulence and so on, our data showed they would not even get to the Philippines."

But the *Voyager I* successfully completed its flight and touched down safely on December 23, 1986. Rutan donated it to the Smithsonian Institution, and then moved on to new challenges. In 1982 he founded another company, Scaled Composites Inc., which was an aerospace prototype development firm. It created prototype models for new aircraft, but Rutan also took on other interesting jobs that required solving aerodynamics challenges. He designed an eighty-five-foot rigid sail that was used on the winning yacht in the 1988 America's Cup race. In 1992 he created an "Ultralite" show car for General Motors Corporation, which was made of lightweight plastics composites. In 1996 he rolled out the Boomerang, a unique asymmetrical twin-engine plane capable of speeds of three hundred miles per hour. He designed an adjustable-wing aircraft capable of high altitudes, called the Proteus, which made its first flight on July 26, 1999.

Became the first company in space

Rutan spent the next several years working on a new pet project, which he called *SpaceShipOne*. It was funded by Paul Allen (1953–), a co-founder of Microsoft, and cost an estimated $20 million. *SpaceShipOne* was a passenger rocket that could be carried aloft by a larger plane, also built by Rutan and his company, called the *White Knight*. The passenger rocket and its test pilot could then be launched into space once it reached a certain altitude.

Rutan and Allen were trying to win the Ansari X Prize with *SpaceShipOne*. The new aviation challenge had been announced in 1996, and had a deadline of January 1, 2005. A $10 million award would be given to the first privately funded group to fulfill the following requirements: that their craft hold three people, reach the 62.5-mile-high sub-orbital flight, and repeat the launch again within a two-week period. Sub-orbital space is where the laws of gravity that govern Earth's physical properties end and weightlessness begins.

Rutan's longtime dream of conquering space with one of his planes came true on June 21, 2004. Mike Melvill, a pilot and employee of Rutan's, climbed aboard *SpaceShipOne,* which was then launched by the *White Knight.* After a successful flight, the plane landed safely on an airstrip at the Mojave Airport. Melvill told reporters at a press

Aircraft designer Burt Rutan's privately-funded spacecraft flies upside down over Mojave, California, April 18, 2003. AP/Wide World Photos. Reproduced by permission.

conference immediately afterward that he had been able to see the curve of Earth, and that he also tossed some M&M candies he had carried aboard in his pocket. He was delighted to see them spin in front of him instead of dropping, since the laws of gravity no longer applied. This was the first successful test flight of a privately funded spacecraft, and made headlines around the world that day.

Imagined ultimate daredevil ride

Rutan watched the successful *SpaceShipOne* voyage from the ground in Mojave. He hoped that a new niche in adventure travel would begin thanks to his company's extraordinary feat. He imagined that space tourists might pay to visit "a kind of astronauts' training school, if you will," as he explained to *Daily News* writer Deborah Hastings. "In some place like Cancun. It would be like a regular two-week vacation with great food and things to do at night. It's kind of like a ride at Magic Mountain…. It isn't just a roller coaster ride. You are officially added to the list of astronauts."

Much of Rutan's work takes place at hangars near his unique pyramid-shaped home in Mojave, California. After the notorious disasters that occurred on two U.S. space shuttle flights, he was even more firmly convinced that his company's planes would serve the twenty-first century's next generation of pioneers. "Entrepreneurs developed the airplane," he reminded *New York Times* journalist Andrew Pollack, "not governments."

For More Information

Books

Encyclopedia of World Biography Supplement. Vol. 20. Detroit, MI: Gale Group, 2000.

Periodicals

Bailey, John. "Rutan's Racer Has Wraps Removed." *Flight International* (April 10, 1991): p. 5.

Bigelow, Bruce V. "Rocket Plane Source of Pride for Designer, Poway, Calif., Firm." Knight Ridder/Tribune Business News (December 18, 2003): p. ITEM03352173.

Bigelow, Bruce V. "San Diego-Area Aircraft Designer Has a Qwest to Bring Space within Reach." Knight Ridder/Tribune Business News (April 29, 2003): p. ITEM03119032 .

Bostwick, Charles F. "Rutan Unveils Privately Funded Spacecraft." *Daily News* (Los Angeles) (April 19, 2003): p. N1.

Carreau, Mark. "Privately-Financed Team Will Try to Send Man into Space." Knight Ridder/Tribune Business News (June 3, 2004): p. ITEM04155061.

Costello, Carol and Miles O'Brien. "The Rutan Brothers." *America's Intelligence Wire* (from CNN News) (December 17, 2003). This article can also be found online at http://www.cnn.com/TRANSCRIPTS/0312/17/lad.12.html.

Hastings, Deborah. "Iconoclast of Aircraft Design Refuses to Work by the Book." *Daily News* (Los Angeles, CA) (July 8, 1996): p. SC1.

Lemonick, Michael D. "Voyager's Triumph; A Flying Fuel Tank Sets Records." *Time* (July 28, 1986): p. 53.

Meisler, Andy. "Slipping the Bonds of Earth and Sky." *New York Times* (August 3, 1995): p. C1.

O'Brien, Miles, Bruce Burkhardt, and Kathleen Koch. "Wright Stuff; A Century of Flight-Part 1." *America's Intelligence Wire* (from CNN News) (December 13, 2003). This article can also be found online at http://www.cnn.com/TRANSCRIPTS/0312/13/nac.00.html.

Park, Edwards. "The Voyager's Bid to Girdle the Globe Is No Mere Canard." *Smithsonian* (February 1985): p. 72.

"Pilot Guides Private Plane Out of Atmosphere, a First." *New York Times* (June 21, 2004).

Pollack, Andrew. "A Maverick's Agenda: Nonstop Global Flight and Tourists in Space." *New York Times* (December 9, 2003): p. G5.

"Private Rocket Plane Unveiled by Burt Rutan." *Advanced Materials & Composites News* (May 5, 2003).

Schwartz, John. "Private Space Travel? Dreamers Hope a Catalyst Will Rise from the Mojave Desert." *New York Times* (June 14, 2004).

Skeen, Jim. "Private Spaceship Makes Supersonic Flight from Mojave, Calif., Airport." Knight Ridder/Tribune Business News (December 18, 2003): p. ITEM03352038.

Stone, Brad. "Let's Go to Space! One Hundred Years After the Wright Brothers' Famous Flight, a New Breed of Entrepreneur Is Pushing New Technologies to Their Limits, Turning Science Fiction into Reality." *Newsweek* (October 6, 2003): p. 54.

Sugar, Jim. "Boomerang!" *Popular Mechanics* (November 1996): p. 50.

"Tier One: Rutan Enters the Space Race with a Radical Design Now in Testing." *Popular Science* (December 1, 2003): p. 42.

Josh Schwartz

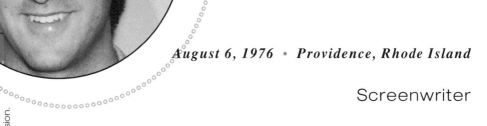

August 6, 1976 • Providence, Rhode Island

Screenwriter

The Fox network introduced *The O.C.* in August of 2003 as something of an experiment. The television show about a high school kid from the wrong side of the tracks who moves into the ultra-posh world of Orange County, California, seemed like a soap opera long shot. Critics predicted *The O.C.* would be another Fox clunker, and doubted that the show would make it past its first seven episodes. Audiences proved them wrong. After the very first episode, fans of all ages were hooked, and soon Fox had a runaway hit on its hands. Some chalked up the show's success to its good-looking cast, but most realized that the true star was Josh Schwartz, *The O.C.'s* hip, young creator and executive producer. When his show hit the small screen, Schwartz, at twenty-six, was the youngest person ever to create a one-hour drama for network television.

Tons and tons of movies

The writer who captures life in southern California week after week for television was actually raised, along with his two younger brothers, in Rhode Island. Josh Schwartz was born August 6, 1976, in Providence, Rhode Island, to Stephen and Honey Schwartz. Josh may have gotten some of his early interest in popular culture from his father, since Stephen Schwartz was a toy inventor and president of Hasbro's Playskool division.

Growing up, Schwartz spent most of his time watching movies, "tons of movies," according to brother Dan, who spoke with Suzanne Ryan of the *Boston Globe*. "I remember him sitting in his room all the time, quoting lines and doing impersonations. He could tell you anything about any movie." By the seventh grade, Schwartz was writing scripts that focused on the lives of his friends. He also proved he had a

> **"I'm not a teen but I'm not 50 either. I remember distinctly what it was like to be 16."**

knack for acting, appearing in such school plays as *You're a Good Man, Charlie Brown* and *Amadeus*. Schwartz attended the Wheeler School, a private, progressive school in Providence. He was so good in Wheeler productions that he attracted a following. As one of his former neighbors told Ryan, "My daughters and I used to call ourselves the Joshettes. We were his fan club. He had so much charisma."

After graduating from Wheeler in 1995, Schwartz packed up his bags and headed for the West Coast, the land where movies are made. "The thought of coming to Southern California, to Hollywood, was incredibly intoxicating," Schwartz explained to Jiby Kattakayam in a 2004 interview. "It was always my dream to come here." Schwartz enrolled at the University of Southern California (USC) School of Cinema-Television, a famous film school whose alumni include such Hollywood heavyweights as directors Ron Howard (1954–) and George Lucas (1944–).

From USC to *The O.C.*

Schwartz thrived in the creative environment of USC, spending time with fellow students who loved the movies just as much as he did. He was also an incredibly dedicated student, who earned high praise from his professors. "I thought he was exceptional," Schwartz's writing teacher told Suzanne Ryan. He was so exceptional that the first screenplay he wrote at USC won the school's Jack Nicholson Scholarship Award, named after American actor Jack Nicholson (1937–). Schwartz was thrilled, especially since the scholarship award was for $5,000. Unfortunately, the scholarship was taken away because he had not read the fine print: only students who were juniors or above could enter, and Schwartz was just a sophomore.

The screenplay, called *Providence,* was based on Schwartz's own experiences as a high school senior in Rhode Island. He shopped the script around, and the executives at Columbia Pictures bit. At the beginning of his junior year, Columbia purchased Schwartz's script for close to $1 million. The script was never made into a movie, but it did open doors for the young filmmaker, who decided to quit school and go to work. Schwartz zeroed in on television, and sold several pilots, which are samples of television shows, to ABC and the WB. He also talked with Fox about creating a television series that would focus on working at a New York gossip magazine. Again, nothing came of the scripts, but Schwartz had caught the attention of Fox executives.

Schwartz had been developing a fish-out-of-water script based on how he felt as a student from Rhode Island meeting the California culture. Fox liked the idea, and Schwartz fleshed out the show's concept with Joseph McGinty Nichol, known as McG (1969–), director of the *Charlie's Angels* movies. McG, like Schwartz, was not a California native. He originally hailed from Michigan, but grew up in Newport Beach, in Orange County. Part of McG's goal in working on *The O.C.,* was to accurately portray what it feels like to be an outsider.

Another *Beverly Hills 90210*?

Fox approved the project in spring 2003 and placed a lot of trust in the untried writer. One reason is that they hoped to strike gold a second time with younger audiences. The network had scored an enormous hit during the 1990s with the long-running teen drama *Beverly Hills 90210,* which centered on a brother and sister from Minnesota who are transplanted to glitzy Beverly Hills. *The O.C.* had the same sort of feel. As Peter Johnson, a Fox senior vice president, explained to Ryan,

Adam Brody: America's Favorite Geek

When *The O.C.* first premiered, most of the press focused on actor Benjamin McKenzie, and the character he played on the show, brooding rebel Ryan Atwood. McKenzie, a newcomer to Hollywood, was applauded by critics for his cool, understated acting. People even compared him to 1950s acting legend, James Dean (1931–1955). Girls thought he looked like a young Cameron Crowe (1957–), and everyone predicted there was a new heartthrob in town. As more episodes aired, however, the character of Seth, Sandy and Kirsten Cohen's geeky son, started to draw more of our attention. He was quirky, he delivered great one-liners, and he was adorable. As a result, the spotlight started shifting from Benjamin McKenzie to Adam Brody, the actor who plays Seth.

Adam Brody was born on April 8, 1981, in San Diego, California. While growing up, Brody spent much of his time at the beach, swimming and surfing. At one point, he actually thought about becoming a professional surfer. However, in the back of his mind, his secret dream was to become an actor. One day, while floating on his surfboard, he devised a plan to make his dream come true. Brody talked his parents into letting him go to college in Los Angeles. He moved to L.A. in 1999, but instead of taking college courses, he hired an acting coach and starting auditioning for roles on television and in film. Within a year, Brody snagged the lead in the television movie *Growing Up Brady,* playing actor Barry Williams (1954–), star of the popular TV series *The Brady Bunch.*

Following *Growing Up Brady,* Brody had bit parts in films such as *American Pie 2* (2001) and *The Ring* (2002). He also gained his first minor success on the WB television show, *Gilmore Girls,* playing David Rygalsky during the 2002–03 season. In 2003, when he was cast in *The O.C.,* Brody had more experience than his

"We've been wanting to do something that harkens back to the success of '90210' and do it in a way that is obviously contemporary. Josh has a voice that feels authentic.… He really is a big talent."

The O.C. was slated to debut in late summer. As a result, Schwartz worked night and day to pound out twenty-seven episodes. He was helped by a staff of six writers who locked themselves in a room to sketch out characters and break down storylines. They also had to cast the show. Directors ultimately went with new faces, although one of the show's stars is veteran actor Peter Gallagher (1955–), who plays public defender Sandy Cohen, the father at the heart of *The O.C.*

In the pilot episode, Cohen brings home one of his clients, sixteen-year-old Ryan Atwood who has nowhere else to go. Cohen and his wife, Kirsten, a real-estate developer, live in swanky Newport Beach, Orange County; Ryan is from, to quote one of the show's teen characters, "Chino, ew." Although he was arrested for stealing a car, younger co-stars, but he was still relatively unknown. That fact would soon change as the press started to knock at his door. It seemed that Brody had a lot of fans who wanted to know more about the dark-haired actor and his alter-ego, Seth Cohen. But where does Seth Cohen begin and Adam Brody leave off?

"As the show goes on, Seth is becoming more like me," Brody told Maxine Shen of Fox News. "I like to think I'm steadier on my feet with girls, but other than that, we're into the same things." Brody credits the show's creator, Josh Schwartz, for integrating real-life Brody-isms into his *O.C.* character. For example, Brody constantly says "dude," and Schwartz began writing that in to Seth's dialogue. Seth was originally supposed to love sailing, but when Brody told Schwartz he would have a lot more fun surfing, surfboards appeared in Seth's bedroom. Brody's favorite band is Death Cab for Cutie, and in one episode Seth is listening to one of their songs. And, Seth, like Brody, is definitely into comic books.

Adam Brody of **The O.C.** AP/Wide World Photos. Reproduced by permission.

Ryan is not a criminal. He is a sensitive soul, wise beyond his years, who just happens to live in the wrong zip code. Ryan tries to fit in with the pampered set, but it is an uphill battle. His hot temper puts him at odds with the resident jock, Luke Ward. Atwood eventually bonds with Seth Cohen, the dorky, comic-book-loving son, and there are romantic sparks between him and beautiful, yet troubled, girl-next-door Marissa Cooper.

Best TV of 2003

The O.C. debuted on Tuesday, August 5, 2003, and viewers tuned in. It was the twenty-seventh most-watched television program in the United States and was Fox's highest-rated show. Critics either loved it or hated it. Some, like Tom Shales of the *Washington Post,* dismissed it as a predictable drama "about rich young brats," and prayed that it would be cancelled. Others, like James Poniewozik of *Time,* agreed that the show followed the predictable formula of a soap opera, complete with pretty people, flashy clothes, and high drama. But, as Poniewozik observed, the formula was delivered with "so much style and believability that it feels new again."

The O.C. rose steadily in the ratings, and by September it had reached number one. Fox briefly took it off the air until after the major league baseball playoffs, but the fan base was so strong that viewers waited patiently for its return at the end of October. Web sites devoted to the show sprang up by the thousands, and the show's young stars became overnight celebrities. By the end of 2003, *The O.C.* was an undisputed hit. It was named one of the ten best shows of the year by *Entertainment Weekly* magazine, and *Time* included the teen soap in its 2003 "Best of TV" list.

However, it seemed that not just teens were tuning in to watch Seth, Ryan, and Marissa. Young viewers were hooked, but so were their parents. According to Hal Boedeker of the *Orlando Sentinel,* the reason why *The O.C.* was so successful, why it was different, was not just because of the hip dialogue and the hunky stars. The appeal was that the show "manages to make the adults every bit as compelling as the teens." Sandy Cohen does not just disappear after he brings Ryan home to Newport Beach. He is an integral part of the storylines, a laid-back father who plays video games with his kids and surfs to clear his head. As Schwartz told Boedeker, "There's a lot of my dad in that character. There's a lot of Peter Gallagher in the character. Both guys are really wonderful fathers. They have a sense of humor and get it. Sandy gets it.… He's cool. He's compassionate."

Schwartz's clear vision

The first season of the *The O.C.* ended in May of 2004, and the Fox network was only too happy to pick up the show for a second season. Fox executives gave Schwartz all the credit. In interviews, however, the young man from Rhode Island was quick to acknowledge the contributions of director McG, and his staff of writers, most of whom were seasoned veterans. Marcy Ross, Fox senior vice president, insisted Schwartz was behind the show's popularity. As she explained to Boedeker, the reason for *The O.C.'s* success is Schwartz's clear vision: "He never wavers from it. That's why the show has captured the imagination of so many young people."

Schwartz has also never wavered from the goal he had growing up. According to his father, Stephen, who spoke with Suzanne Ryan in 2003, "Josh has known he wanted to be a screenwriter since he was eight years old." Less than twenty years later, Schwartz had achieved his goal. At the age of twenty-six, he created his first television program. At twenty-seven, he was the driving force behind a television phenomenon."

For More Information

Periodicals

Boedeker, Hal. "'O.C.' Creator Schwartz Adds Laugh, Lust and Love to Hit Show." *Orlando Sentinel* (April 20, 2004).

Chocano, Carina. "Orange Crush: Welcome to the O.C." *Entertainment Weekly* (August 15, 2004): p. 61.

Poniewozik, James. "The Same Young Story: The Appealing Teen Drama 'The O.C.' Proves That Piling on Soap-Opera Cliches Isn't Always a Bad Thing." *Time* (August 11, 2003).

Ryan, Suzanne C. "At 26, Josh Schwartz Is Living His Childhood Goal in L.A. as Creator of Fox's New Teen Drama." *Boston Globe* (August 5, 2003): p. E1.

Shales, Tom. "'The O.C.': Land of the Brooding Teen." *Washington Post* (August 5, 2003): p. C01.

Web Sites

Kattakayam, Jiby. "Josh Schwartz Interview." *USC CN-TV Web site.* (March 11, 2004). http://www.cntvalumni.net/displaypost.cfm?PostType=AlumNews&PostingID=1861 (accessed on May 30, 2004).

The O.C. Web site. http://www.fox.com/oc (accessed on May 30, 2004).

"'The O.C.': Television Review." *PopMatters Web site.* (November 4, 2003). http://www.popmatters.com/tv/reviews/o/oc.shtml (accessed on May 30, 2004).

Shen, Maxine. "Adam Brody Talks about Being the Nerd of 'The O.C.'" *Fox News: Fox Life.* (September 17, 2003).http://www.foxnews.com/story/0,2933,97551,00.html (accessed on May 30, 2004).

Arnold Schwarzenegger

July 30, 1947 · *Graz, Austria*

Actor, politician, bodybuilder

Most people successfully pursue one or two careers throughout their lives. By the age of fifty-six, Arnold Schwarzenegger had tackled at least three—bodybuilding, acting, and politics. It is difficult to break into any one of these professions, yet Schwarzenegger managed to excel in each and every one. He earned thirteen world bodybuilding championships, is considered one of the most influential actors in Hollywood, and, in 2003, without ever running for political office before, he became the governor of California. If Schwarzenegger had listened to his many critics along the way, he never would have succeeded. However, with discipline, determination, and drive, he proved that an Austrian-born immigrant can achieve the American dream.

The need to succeed

Arnold Alois Schwarzenegger was born on July 30, 1947, the second son of Gustav and Aurelia Schwarzenegger. He was raised, along with older brother Meinhard, in the tiny village of Thal, just outside of Graz,

Austria. Schwarzenegger's father, Gustav, was the local police chief, and the family lived above the police station where Gustav worked. The Schwarzenegger home was a humble one. In fact, they did not have indoor plumbing until Arnold was a teenager. This was not uncommon at the time, however, since families all over Europe were just beginning to recover from the effects of World War II (1939–45).

Before joining the police force, Gustav Schwarzenegger was a military officer, and he ran his household in strict military fashion. Both Arnold and Meinhard were required to get up before sunrise to tend to their chores. After chores came a rigorous exercise routine, followed by breakfast. Gustav also instilled a love of sports in his

> "I learned something from all these years of lifting and training hard.... What I learned was that we are always stronger than we know."

sons. Meinhard, who died when he was twenty-three years old in a car accident, was a boxing champion. Arnold showed promise as a soccer player. It was while performing exercises to strengthen his legs for soccer that Schwarzenegger turned to the sport that would eventually make him famous: bodybuilding.

Arnold Schwarzenegger pursued weightlifting and bodybuilding with a passion. He trained for hours a day, both at a local gym and at home where he set up a training area in a room that had no heat. He also studied anatomy and nutrition to understand how to become physically fit. His parents worried that he was obsessed with training, but Schwarzenegger had his eyes on a goal; that goal was to leave his little village behind and become a success in America.

Mr. Universe

In 1965, after he graduated from high school, Schwarzenegger joined the Austrian army. Just one month after enlisting, he won his first

The Ronald Reagan Comparison

Arnold Schwarzenegger was not the first celebrity to hold public office. For example, professional wrestler Jesse "The Body" Ventura (1951–) was governor of Minnesota from 1998 until 2002, and from 1986 to 1988 actor/director Clint Eastwood (1930–) was mayor of Carmel, California. The best-known celebrity-turned-politician, however, may be Ronald Reagan (1911–2004), former governor of California (1967–1975) and president of the United States (1981–1989). Throughout his run for governor, Schwarzenegger was constantly compared to Reagan for some obvious reasons: both were actors, both were very charismatic speakers, and both were new to politics when they ran for office. But, are there other similarities?

Arnold Schwarzenegger poses with a bronze bust of President Ronald Reagan. Mike Guastella/WireImage.com.

- **Age:** Schwarzenegger and Reagan were both fifty-six years old when they became governor of California.

- **Nicknames:** Reagan was known as "The Great Communicator" while Schwarzenegger was dubbed "The Oak" because of his strength and concentration.

- **Sports:** Both men shared a love of sports and got their start in the world of athletics. Schwarzenegger was a bodybuilder; Reagan played football and was a swimmer. Reagan also got his first break into show business as an announcer for football and baseball games in Iowa.

bodybuilding title, Mr. Junior Europe. The competition was held in Germany, and Schwarzenegger had left his army base without permission to compete. As a result, he spent the next year in the brig, which is a holding area for people in the military who have committed offenses. After he was released, Schwarzenegger resumed his training with gusto, often spending up to five hours a day in the gym.

His grueling schedule paid off in 1967, when, at the age of twenty, Schwarzenegger won his first Mr. Universe title. The Mr. Universe competition is an annual event sponsored by the National Amateur Bodybuilders Association (NABBA). Competitors are judged on such things as size and definition of muscles, balance and proportion of body parts, and overall presentation. The youngest person to ever win the competition, Schwarzenegger was confident that he would keep his title the following year. He was also excited because his dream of traveling to the United States was about to come true since the 1968 Mr. Universe competition was to be held in Miami, Florida.

Although he did not win the 1968 title in Miami, Schwarzenegger was noticed by fitness pioneer Joe Weider (1922–). Weider was so impressed by the young bodybuilder that he invited him to stay in the United States and live and train with him in Los Angeles, California. Schwarzenegger jumped at the chance. Weider became Schwarzenegger's mentor, and from the late 1960s through the 1970s, Schwarzenegger devoted himself to training and competing. He reclaimed his Mr. Universe crown in 1969, and went on to dominate every major bodybuilding competition, including Mr. Universe, Mr. World, and Mr. Olympia.

In addition to being a star bodybuilder, Schwarzenegger helped popularize the sport. He wrote articles about his unique training methods for Weider's fitness magazines; he also was featured in a 1977 documentary about bodybuilding competitions, called *Pumping Iron.* The documentary was quite popular and gave Schwarzenegger his first taste of Hollywood celebrity. In 1980, at the age of thirty-three, he officially retired from bodybuilding to devote himself to a new career: acting.

Box-office gold

Schwarzenegger made a few low-budget movies in the 1970s, cast mostly in small roles that required big muscles, not big talent. In 1982 he was tapped to play the lead in *Conan the Barbarian,* based on the comic-book hero of the same name. Again, Schwarzenegger's strength was in his biceps, not his acting skills. Critics panned his performance, claiming that it was nearly impossible to understand his German-accented English. Audiences, however, loved the movie, which turned out to be a box-office hit. Two years later, in 1984, Schwarzenegger cemented his box-office appeal when he appeared in the movie *The Terminator.*

In *The Terminator,* Schwarzenegger played a violent cyborg (part robot, part human) who is sent from the future to exterminate the mother of humankind's future leader. He spoke seventy-four words in the movie, all delivered in a monotone, robotic voice. Audiences did not mind the lack of acting ability, and they flocked to see Schwarzenegger in the sci-fi thriller. The movie was so popular that Schwarzenegger became known for his character's famous one-liner: "I'll be back," or as Schwarzenegger pronounced it, "Awl be buck."

Action movies like *The Terminator* proved to be wildly popular with people of all ages, and Schwarzenegger proved to be the perfect action hero. He followed *The Terminator* with a string of movies, including *Commando* (1985), *Predator* (1987), *Total Recall* (1990), and *True Lies* (1994). He also continued the Terminator movies, starring in *Terminator 2: Judgment Day* (1991), which produced the famous line, "Hasta la vista, baby," and *Terminator 3: Rise of the Machines* (2003). For his role in *Terminator 3*, Schwarzenegger was paid $30 million.

In addition to playing the tough-as-nails hero, Schwarzenegger starred in a number of comedies, including three movies made by director Ivan Reitman (1946–): *Twins* (1988), *Kindergarten Cop* (1990), and *Junior* (1994). Moviegoers embraced the "lighter side of Arnold," and critics admitted that Schwarzenegger was growing as an actor. Everyone agreed that he was box-office gold. In fact, in 1993, he was recognized as the International Box Office Star of the Decade.

By 2004 Schwarzenegger had appeared in nearly thirty movies, and he brought his unique style to each role. One thing he never lost was his accent. Comedians and critics made countless jokes about the way "Ah-nuld" talked, but Schwarzenegger seemed to take it in stride. He also explained in a 1991 interview with Pat Broeske that he did not want to get rid of his accent completely because it had become, Broeske noted, "his trademark, his signature."

The family man

Schwarzenegger's trademark made him a very wealthy actor, and he used his money wisely, investing in real estate and several businesses, including the restaurant chain Planet Hollywood. He was also a devoted family man. Schwarzenegger met his wife, television journalist Maria Shriver (1955–), in 1977. The couple married in 1986; they

Arnold Schwarzenegger supports Willie McKinney during the bench press competition of the 1999 Special Olympics World Games. AP/ Wide World Photos. Reproduced by permission.

have four children, two boys and two girls. Shriver was no stranger to celebrity, considering she is part of one of the most famous families in the United States. Her mother, Eunice Kennedy Shriver (1921–), is the sister of U.S. president John F. Kennedy (1917–1963).

Most people thought that the couple made a very odd pair. He was a brawny bodybuilder turned actor. She was a "brain" who graduated from Georgetown University in Washington, D.C., and was co-anchor of *CBS Morning News*. He was a well-known supporter of the Republican Party. The Republican Party is considered to be the more conservative of the two major political parties in the United States.

Shriver, as part of the Kennedy clan, was a Democrat to the core. Members of the Democratic Party are traditionally considered to be more liberal. Those closest to the couple, however, say they are a perfect match. Both have competitive drives; both are committed to their family; and both share a wacky sense of humor.

The Schwarzeneggers also share a commitment to politics and to social causes. Since 1979 they have been devoted to the Special Olympics, helping to raise funds and awareness. Established by Eunice Shriver in 1968, Special Olympics provides year-round sports training and sponsors annual athletic competitions for children and adults with mental retardation. There are Special Olympics programs in almost 150 countries; Arnold serves as the Special Olympics International Weight Training Coach.

In 1990 Schwarzenegger was given an incredible opportunity to spread his message about the importance of fitness when President George H. W. Bush (1924–) appointed him chairman of the President's Council on Physical Fitness and Sports (PCPFS). According to the PCPFS Web site, the goal of the council is to "promote, encourage and motivate Americans of all ages to become physically active and participate in sports." Schwarzenegger was the perfect spokesman. With high energy and unlimited enthusiasm, he traveled across the country spreading the word that it was "hip to be fit." When Democrat Bill Clinton (1946–) took over the presidency in 1993, Schwarzenegger resigned from the council.

The "Collectionator"

Schwarzenegger had been such a dynamic public figure in the Bush administration that people wondered if he was heading for a future in politics. Schwarzenegger denied the rumors for years, claiming he was too busy being a businessman and family man. In 2002, however, he spent a good deal of time campaigning in California for state grant money to fund after-school programs for children. And, in 2003, when California governor Gray Davis (1942–) was threatened by a recall, the buzz was strong that Schwarzenegger would throw his hat in the ring.

The year 2003 was a strange one in California politics. Democrat Gray Davis, who had over twenty years of experience in politics, was governor, and had been since 1998. Throughout his first term in office, however, Davis faced a number of problems, including an out-of-control budget, a sagging state economy, and electricity blackouts that left most of the state without power for some time during 2001. Californians were not happy, and they blamed Davis for the sad state of affairs. In 2002, just months into his second term of office, citizens started a campaign to recall Davis as governor. This meant that Davis, through a special election, would possibly be replaced.

The election led to media frenzy since it was the first time in California's history that a governor faced a recall. In addition, people came out of the woodwork to campaign for Davis's job. On August 6, 2003, Schwarzenegger fueled the frenzy by announcing that he, too, was going to run for governor. He made his announcement during an interview on the late-night television program *The Tonight Show.*

Schwarzenegger spent the next several months campaigning in rather untraditional ways. For example, he chatted with Oprah Winfrey (1954–) on her afternoon talk show, and he was interviewed by disc jockey Howard Stern (1954–), who is known for his outrageous radio antics. Schwarzenegger peppered his interviews with references to his movies, promising to say "Hasta la vista" to new taxes and calling himself the "Collectionator," since one of his goals was to ask the federal government for funds to bail California out of its economic crisis.

Arnold to the rescue

All of the media attention prompted voters to turn out in droves, and on October 8, 2003, the citizens of California elected Arnold Schwarzenegger governor with 48.6 percent of the vote. On November 17, during his swearing-in ceremony, Schwarzenegger commented, "It is no secret that I'm a newcomer to politics. I realize I was elected on faith and hope. And I feel a great responsibility not to let the people down."

The public may have felt they needed an action hero to come to their aid, but political commentators had their doubts. Schwarzenegger was able to campaign on catchy phrases, but what would he do once in office? According to political consultant David Axelrod in a 2003 *Time* article, "This isn't the movies. No one is going to throw him a ray gun so he can blow up the deficit."

Schwarzenegger's first days in office were watched closely. He made good on several of his campaign promises, including lowering car taxes. He was also applauded for trying to get California Democrats and Republicans to work together to help solve the state's budget problems. Schwarzenegger, however, was just beginning to flex his political muscles. His state still faced a staggering amount of debt, and he tried to figure a way out without hurting social programs like education and health care.

In March 2004, voters passed Schwarzenegger's Proposition 57, which would allow the state to use bonds (low-interest, long-term loans) to slash $15 billion from the ever-growing debt. Politicians considered the proposition to be a daring move, but Schwarzenegger was used to taking chances, and he had faith that the voters would believe in him. In a rally held just after the vote, and reported on CNN, he reassured the public that his borrowing plan would "make California the golden state that it once was."

Just months into office, people began to speculate once again what was next for Arnold Schwarzenegger, family man, businessman, actor, and now governor. When he appeared on the television program *Meet the Press,* in February 2004, host Tim Russert wondered if perhaps Schwarzenegger had his eye on the White House. Schwarzenegger shooed away the question, commenting that he had been too busy tackling California's problems to think about his next move. "I have no idea," he commented, "I haven't thought about that at all."

But, can we believe him, since that is exactly what Schwarzenegger said when asked if he would ever run for political office? He faces one big obstacle, however. According to the U.S. Constitution, only citizens who were born in the United States are eligible to be president. Although Schwarzenegger became a citizen in 1983, he was born in Austria. A change, or amendment, to the constitution has been proposed that would make it possible for anyone who has been a U.S. citizen for at least twenty years to seek the presidency. And, as Ah-nuld has proven time and again, anything is possible.

For More Information

Periodicals

Boss, Suzie. "Hey, Kids, Get Physical!" *Newsweek* (August 27, 1990): pp. 62–64.

Broeske, Pat H. "Arnold Schwarzenegger." *Interview* (July 1991): p. 85.

Streisand, Betsy. "Reality Check: Effect of Arnold Schwarzenegger's Government." *U.S. News & World Report* (January 12, 2004): p. 26.

Tresniowski, Alex, et al. "What Makes Them Run?" *People Weekly* (August 25, 2003): pp. 50–58.

Tumulty, Karen, and Terry McCarthy. "All That's Missing Is the Popcorn." *Time* (August 18, 2003): pp. 22–30.

Web Sites

Russert, Tim. "Interview with Arnold Schwarzenegger and Ralph Nader." *NBC News' Meet the Press* (February 22, 2004). http://msnbc.msn.com/id/4304155 (accessed on May 30, 2004).

Schwarzenegger.com: The Official Web site. http://www.schwarzenegger.com (accessed on May 30, 2004).

"Schwarzenegger's Inauguration Speech." *CNN.com: Inside Politics.* http://www.cnn.com/2003/ALLPOLITICS/11/17/arnold.speech (accessed on May 31, 2004).

"Schwarzenegger Wins Budget Test." *CNN.com: Inside Politics* (March 3, 2004). http://www5.cnn.com/2004/ALLPOLITICS/03/03/california.proposition.ap (accessed on May 30, 2004).

Ryan Seacrest

December 24, 1974 • *Atlanta, Georgia*

Entertainer

Ryan Seacrest's career did not begin on *American Idol,* but the popularity of the televised talent search contest on Fox helped make him a household name by 2003. Before taking the *American Idol* job, Seacrest hosted a highly rated radio show in Los Angeles that dominated the afternoon drive-time slot. His career began to flourish in 2004 with the debut of his daily daytime television show, *On-Air with Ryan Seacrest.*

High school DJ

Born in 1974, Seacrest grew up in Dunwoody, Georgia, where his father, Gary, was a lawyer. He was an overweight child, teased by others, and preferred to stay indoors listening to the radio. His fascination with the medium evolved into making his own radio show tapes, and he would give the cassettes to his parents to play in their cars. "I thought it was a hobby," his homemaker mother, Connie, told Allison

Glock in a *New York Times Magazine* profile. "But people would call my answering machine just to listen to his voice. They thought I had a professional doing it. That's when I thought, This might be bigger than I think it is."

At age fourteen Seacrest became the "Voice of Dunwoody High School," as his school's regular morning public-address system announcer. He was still anything but a star there, he told another *New York Times* writer, Hilary De Vries. "I wore braces and glasses and was fat and got teased about it," Seacrest said, "but I was always very ambitious." He eventually lost weight by cutting out nearly everything in his school lunch except for the oranges his mother had packed for him. In

> " Ryan has the appeal of a dog that has been rescued from the pound. That is his secret. He's grateful. He's happy. Always, always. If he had a tail, he'd wag it. "
>
> **Simon Cowell, *New York Times Magazine*, May 23, 2004.**

1991, the year he became a junior at Dunwoody High, he landed a hard-to-get internship at Atlanta pop music station WSTR-FM.

One night the regular DJ called in sick and asked Seacrest to take his shift. Both thought the station owner was out of town, but he wasn't, and Seacrest received a surprise telephone call on the studio hotline during his live debut. Assuming he would be fired, he went to see his boss the next day in order to apologize. Instead, the station owner told Seacrest that, though he was not a professional, his stint of the night before hadn't been too bad. The boss offered to start training him, and soon Seacrest was given the weekend overnight shift at WSTR.

Headed for Hollywood

After graduating from Dunwoody High in 1993, Seacrest stayed at the station and began taking journalism classes at the University of Geor-

British *Pop Idol* Hosts

Ryan Seacrest has hosted *American Idol* since its debut in 2002, but the show is a remake of a British hit that premiered in the fall of 2001. The ITV Network's *Pop Idol* also featured Simon Cowell as a judge, but it was hosted by a pair of English comedians named Ant and Dec. Unlike Seacrest, they were already widely known in their country, thanks to their popular Saturday morning children's show.

Ant and Dec are Anthony McPartlin and Declan Donnelly. Both were born in Newcastle-upon-Tyne in 1975. They met when cast in a British Broadcasting Corporation (BBC) soap opera for teens called *Byker Grove* in 1990. Their characters, PJ and Duncan, were popular, but McPartlin lost his part when the show's writers had him maimed in a freak paintball accident. The two went on to release a series of pop music albums, and in 1995 became hosts of their own short-lived BBC series, *The Ant and Dec Show.* It was followed by *Ant and Dec Unzipped* in 1997, but the two boyish, energetic personalities only hit their stride with *SM:tv Live,* a Saturday morning show aimed at young viewers on ITV. Their antics made them popular with their target audience, but older viewers began tuning in as well. On their show, Ant and Den spoofed the *Byker Grove* paintball episode,

gave away their pop records to guests—joking they still had boxes of them left—and mercilessly teased youngsters who called in to the show.

Ant and Dec hosted *SM:tv* until *Pop Idol* came calling. Like Seacrest, their easy banter and likable personalities provided relief from Cowell's cutting remarks. Once they even played one of their well-planned pranks on Cowell, after the show became a success in the United States as *American Idol*: they donned wigs, fake beards, and prosthetic makeup and auditioned as two of the thousands of hopefuls who tried out.

Ant and Dec are often referred to as Britain's favorite "Geordies," a nickname for those from the north of England, who have a distinct accent. In 2002 they became hosts of *Ant & Dec's Saturday Night Takeaway,* which was set to make its American TV debut in late 2004 on the Fox Network. There were no plans to air the prank they played on Cowell, in which they sang a Paula Abdul song with American accents. "Thank god the American audiences didn't see that," Donnelly told Sam Wonfor and Alison Dargie in the *Journal* of Newcastle, England. "I don't think it would be the best way for us to introduce ourselves to them. Maybe we'll show them one day."

gia. He also made his television debut as host of an ESPN show for kids called *Radical Outdoor Challenge.* When he was nineteen, he quit the Atlanta radio station and moved to Los Angeles, enrolling at Santa Monica College. He had a hard time finding work in the highly competitive radio market in southern California, but he did land some television jobs. He was a weekend anchor on the entertainment-news show *Extra,* and hosted series like *Gladiators,* Sci-Fi Channel's *The New Edge,* and *The Click,* a teen quiz show. He also worked as an overnight radio DJ and eventually took over the drive-time slot on

Ryan Seacrest (left) on stage with **American Idol 2003** *winner Ruben* ***Studdard.*** Steve Granitz/WireImage.com.

KYSR, an alternative music station, with the highly-rated "Ryan Seacrest for the Ride Home."

By 1999 Seacrest's show had become the top-rated Los Angeles-area radio program in its time slot. He continued to take the occasional television job, and in 2002 came under consideration for a seat on the judging panel of a new reality-TV series, *American Idol*. The Fox Network show was based on a hit British series of the previous year called *Pop Idol*. In both shows unknown hopefuls competed for a chance at a record contract, and viewers could phone a special number and cast their votes for their favorite performer that week. One by one, the singers would be eliminated. Simon Cowell (1959–), a British record executive who made the Spice Girls a success, brought the show across the Atlantic. Cowell and others felt that the likable Seacrest might be better suited for the job of host. "They asked if I thought I could handle live TV," he recalled in the interview with Glock, and "I said, 'Of course,' even though I had no idea."

American Idol debuted in the summer of 2002 and was a phenomenal success almost from the start. Seacrest's on-screen enthusiasm made him an overnight sensation, and the show was seen by some twenty-six million viewers weekly. As *American Idol* grew in popularity, Seacrest, Cowell, fellow judges Paula Abdul (1962–) and Randy Jackson (1956–), as well as the final contestants, all became household names. Seacrest was sometimes described as the antidote to Cowell, who often judged the contestants' talents harshly. "I think we're showing that there is more than one way to launch a star," Seacrest said, when De Vries asked him about why *American Idol* had captured the nation's attention. "It could have been a great TV show, but not have any validity in the record-buying world. But we've proven to be very successful that way."

Sometimes Seacrest and Cowell traded insults on the air. Cowell later penned a book on the *American Idol* phenomenon in which he claimed that Seacrest, known for his perfectly coiffed hair, sometimes spent three hours in the hair and makeup room before a taping. "That's a bit of an exaggeration," Seacrest said, when *Atlanta Journal-Constitution* staff writer Rodney Ho asked him about it. "My hair, makeup and wardrobe takes about 14 minutes. I don't have three hours in my life to do anything."

Given daily TV show

Seacrest's schedule became even busier in early 2004, when he began hosting *On-Air with Ryan Seacrest,* a syndicated daytime television talk show. He described its core audience to one interviewer as young adults who had spent their teen years watching MTV's *Total Request Live* and were now ready for more grown-up fare. The show was a mix of entertainment news, in-studio performances by guests like Missy Elliott (1972–), and live performances outside its studio at the Hollywood & Highland complex in Los Angeles, a tourist mecca. The host also bantered with guests like Donald Trump (1946–), and segued to reports from the show's remote correspondents. Fox Television built Seacrest a new studio for the television and radio show of the same name, a facility that cost a reported $10 million. By then, Seacrest was thought to make about that same amount of money yearly.

Around the same time his new television show debuted, Seacrest also began hosting the weekly radio staple *American Top 40*. He replaced longtime host Casey Kasem (1932–), who had retired from the top-rated chart hits countdown show heard on hundreds of radio stations across the United States each week. Kasem had been one of Seacrest's radio idols when he was growing up, along with Dick Clark (1929–), host of the weekly music show *American Bandstand* from

1956 to 1987. Seacrest once asked Clark for some career advice, and Clark told him the business had changed dramatically over the decades. A stake in ownership was important to have, Clark believed, and so Seacrest negotiated a piece of the ownership pie for the televised *On-Air.* He hoped that it might become "a brand name that could live forever," he explained to De Vries. "So maybe in 20 years it will still be called 'On Air,' with someone else hosting the show, but I can still produce it. Because, let's be honest, you don't know how long people are going to let you into their homes."

Seacrest's own home is a three-story Italianate villa in the Hollywood Hills. He began dating actress and singer Shana Wall in 2003, which seemed to put an end to persistent rumors about his sexual orientation. In interviews, he readily admitted he had "metrosexual" tendencies, using the catchphrase of 2003 for straight guys who exhibited some of the stylishness commonly associated with gay men. Well before the metrosexual term came into common usage, Seacrest used to talk on his L.A. radio show about getting his eyebrows waxed. He once confessed to celebutante Paris Hilton that his flatiron was also a cherished possession in his household. "What can I do about it?" he asked *Entertainment Weekly* journalist Nicholas Fonseca, about his love of hairstyling products and well-tailored shirts. "I could lie and pretend that I hunt and camp, but that wouldn't be me. Clothes? Shopping? That's stuff I like!"

For More Information

Periodicals

"£10m Bid for Ant 'n' Dec." *Birmingham Evening Mail* (Birmingham, England) (May 12, 2004): p. 6.

Curtis, Nick. "What Makes These Two the Hottest Stars on TV?" *Evening Standard* (London, England) (October 26, 2001): p. 31.

De Vries, Hilary. "His Feet in 'American Idol,' and Reaching to Be a Star." *New York Times* (January 11, 2004): p. AR30.

Fonseca, Nicholas. "The Music Man: American Idol Host Ryan Seacrest's Blond Ambition Has Earned Him a New Talk Show and Makes Him Hair, We Mean Heir, Apparent to Dick Clark." *Entertainment Weekly* (January 9, 2004): p. 46.

Glock, Allison. "Bland Ambition." *New York Times* (May 23, 2004): p. 20.

Ho, Rodney. "Life of Ryan: Atlanta-Born Ryan Seacrest Hopes His New TV Talk Show, Starting Today, Is the Springboard to a Media Empire." *Atlanta Journal-Constitution* (January 12, 2004): p. B1.

Lipton, Michael A. "Fast Forward: American Idol's Hyper Host Ryan Seacrest Makes Room for Talk TV, a Radio Gig—And Romance." *People* (January 19,2004): p. 69.

Moir, Jan. "'Yes, We Are Rather Middle-Aged.'" *Daily Telegraph* (London, England) (December 6, 2001): p. 22.

"Movie for Ant and Dec." *Evening Chronicle* (April 2, 2004): p. 2.

Poniewozik, James. "Shallow like a Fox: Ryan Seacrest of American Idol and On-Air Hopes to Turn Pop Fluff into an Empire. Go Ahead and Laugh." *Time* (January 26, 2004): p. 62.

Singh, Anita. "Ant and Dec's Audition Fools Pop Idol's Mr Nasty." Europe Intelligence Wire (January 9, 2003).

Wonfor, Sam, and Alison Dargie. "Ant and Dec Bid to Be Idols in US." *Journal* (Newcastle, England) (November 3, 2003): p. 7.

Terry Semel

Arun Nevader/WireImage.com.

February 24, 1943 • *Brooklyn, New York*

CEO, Yahoo! Inc.

Do you Yahoo? Millions of computer users Yahoo every single day, but when Terry Semel took over as chief executive officer (CEO) of Yahoo! Inc. in 2001, he was not one of them. In fact, Semel knew very little about computers. When he received an e-mail, one of his assistants would print it out and Semel would scrawl out a written reply. Nevertheless, when Yahoo, one of the biggest Internet service providers, was struggling to survive in the cutthroat on-line industry, it turned to Semel. His more than thirty-year track record as an entertainment executive was unparalleled. By 2004, after a string of shrewd mergers and a creative organization redesign spearheaded by Semel, Yahoo was back in the game. Its stock prices were on the rise and analysts predicted a healthy future. Semel, the man who had barely ever surfed the Net, was given all the credit.

A bored accountant goes Hollywood

The man who resurrected Yahoo was born on February 24, 1943, in Brooklyn, New York. His father, Benjamin Semel, was a women's coat designer; his mother, Mildred, was an executive at a bus company. In 1964 Semel earned a degree in accounting from Long Island University in Brooklyn, New York. He briefly worked as an accountant, but soon became bored. When a friend told him about a sales training program offered by Warner Brothers, one of the top movie studios in the United States, Semel did not hesitate to change careers. As he explained to Fred Vogelstein of *Fortune* magazine, the Warner program offered him a "chance to learn about marketing and sales,

> **"We're not going to be crushed by anyone but our own ineptitude."**

which I was interested in." Semel simultaneously attended City College of New York in New York City, where he earned a master's degree in business administration (MBA) in 1967.

Semel's early days at Warner were spent on the road as a movie salesman. He traveled across the country with a list of upcoming Warner features, and talked theater owners into buying what hopefully would be the next box-office hit. Semel was such a whiz at sales that he caught the attention of other entertainment companies. In 1971 he became domestic sales manager at CBS-Cinema Center Films. Two years later he was named vice president and general sales manager of Buena Vista, a division of Walt Disney. In 1975 Semel was lured back to where he had begun: Warner Brothers. That same year he met Robert Daly, the man who would become his future business partner.

At first Semel was in charge of Warner distribution. Within five years he and Daly were running the entire studio. In 1982 Semel was named the company's president and chief operating officer (COO). In 1994 he became co-chair and co-chief executive officer (CEO) at Warner, sharing the duties with Daly. From the late 1970s to the late 1990s, Semel and Daly were known as one of the most powerful duos in Hollywood, and were responsible for turning Warner Brothers from a successful movie studio into an entertainment giant. As Vogelstein commented, "The twenty years that Semel and Daly ran Warner will probably go down as one of the longest and most successful partnerships in Hollywood history."

The dynamic duo

In the 1970s, before Semel and Daly took the helm, Warner Brothers was bringing in about $1 billion a year, with most of the studio's revenue coming from its films and its record label, Warner Brothers Music. Semel and Daly changed all that, effectively transforming the way movies were made and marketed, and how studios functioned. The duo expanded Warner Brothers into international markets, extended the music division to include hit record labels such as Elektra and Maverick, and broadened the company's entertainment arm to embrace television. Warner Brothers Television was responsible for producing many popular network TV series, including *China Beach, E.R.,* and *Friends.* In 1995 Semel and Daly went one step beyond and launched the Warner Brothers (WB) Network, which created original series aimed at a younger audience.

Perhaps the most revolutionary thing that Semel and Daly accomplished was to turn Warner Brothers into a brand name. Warner Brothers Studio Stores popped up across the United States and carried all kinds of merchandise, from shirts to hats to neckties featuring well-known Warner Brothers animated characters such as Bugs Bunny, Daffy Duck, and Scooby-Doo. Semel and Daly also saw the potential in movies as merchandise, and began selling various products related to the movies they made. In 1989 they took a chance on an unknown director named Tim Burton (1958–), and brought *Batman* to the big screen. The film was incredibly expensive to make, but it became one of the most successful movies of all time. It was also a merchandising gold mine, setting the standard for the way filmmakers of the future would finance and market their movies.

By the late 1990s, under Semel and Daly's guidance, Warner's annual revenues had grown from $1 billion to approximately $11 billion. The company had expanded as never before, and its film division was in peak form. In addition to *Batman,* Semel and Daly had green-

David Filo and Jerry Yang: Chief Yahoos

Yahoo was founded in 1994 by two friends at Stanford University, David Filo and Jerry Yang. Filo, like Terry Semel, is very quiet and avoids the limelight, rarely giving interviews. Yang is the more outgoing of the two and acts as the company's cheerleader. Both men still take an active part in the company, although Filo prefers to focus on the technology end of things. His title is key technologist. Yang sits on the board of directors and works closely with Semel to direct the company's business focus. The title the two men share and the one they gave themselves is that of Chief Yahoo.

David Filo was born in 1966 in Wisconsin to Jerry and Carol Filo; Jerry was an architect and Carol an accountant. The family soon moved to Moss Bluff, Louisiana, where they lived in an alternative community setting along with several other families. In 1988 Filo earned a bachelor's degree in computer engineering from Tulane University in New Orleans. He then moved to Palo Alto, California, to study at Stanford University, where he met future friend and business partner Jerry Yang.

Yang was born Chih-Yuan Yang in Taiwan in 1968. His father died when he was only two years old and he, along with younger brother, Ken, were raised by his mother, Lily, an English and drama teacher. When Yang was ten, Lily moved her family to the United States, settling in a suburb of San Jose, California. At first Yang spoke only Chinese, but he learned English quickly, and earned straight A's in school. After graduating from high school he attended Stanford where, in 1990, he simultaneously earned bachelor's and master's degrees in electrical engineering.

While they were doctoral students, Filo and Yang shared an office at Stanford. The "office" was a trailer filled with pizza boxes, golf clubs, and dirty laundry. Of course the office also housed their computers, which they nicknamed Akebono and Konishiki, after their favorite Sumo wrestlers. This was in the early days of the Internet, and Filo and Yang were soon hooked on the new technology, often spending hours surfing the Net instead of focusing on their Ph.D. studies. The World Wide Web, however, was difficult to navigate, because it was a mishmash of uncategorized data. Because they used the Internet so much, Filo and Yang decided to create an index of their favorite Web sites, a kind of roadmap that would help them get to their sites more easily. They designed some simple software that organized the Web pages by subject, and they

lighted some four hundred films. Some were blockbusters like the sci-fi thriller *The Matrix* (1999); at least thirteen were nominated for a Best Picture Academy Award; and three actually took home the top honor. Semel and Daly were the toast of Hollywood, and were consistently named to the power lists of the entertainment business.

In 1999, however, the dynamic duo's tenure came to an end. Semel and Daly had survived many twists and turns in the Warner Brothers organization, including the company takeover by Time, Inc., in 1989 and the Time Warner merger with Turner Broadcasting in 1996. But in July of 1999, during contract negotiations, the pair decided to leave the company. Some insiders claimed that they were forced out after a string of launched their own Web site, called "Jerry and David's Guide to the World Wide Web."

Since the Web site resided on the Stanford server, Stanford students quickly began to use the helpful new tool. Other users stumbled on it, and within months the site was attracting thousands of people who were looking for a way to locate their favorite Web pages. Because their site was visited so often, Filo and Yang decided to change the site name to something a little simpler. After searching through the dictionary they found the word *yahoo* and decided to poke fun at themselves, since a yahoo is an unsophisticated person. The newly-named Yahoo continued to attract more users, and began to attract the attention of on-line companies such as America Online (AOL), who offered to buy the service. Filo and Yang, however, retained ownership of their creation, and continued to work up to twenty hours a day to make Yahoo an even better search engine.

In 1995 the pair received backing to start their own company, and a friend from Stanford helped them write a business plan. They left Stanford, rented office space, and in 1996 the company went public, which means that its stock was offered for sale to the public for the first time. Filo and Yang became instant millionaires. They also became examples of the modern-day executive: young, anti-

David Filo (left) and Jerry Yang. © Ed Kashi/Corbis.

corporate entrepreneurs who wore jeans to the office and worked barefoot late into the night. Along the way, Filo and Yang forever changed the way people view the Internet. Yahoo eventually grew from a search engine to becoming an Internet portal for people to access the World Wide Web. Today, Yahoo offers personalized Web pages, e-mail, chat rooms, and message boards. Users can log on to get any kind of information imaginable, from finance reports to a song by a favorite music artist—all in a fun, slick environment. And the thanks go to Filo and Yang, just a couple of Yahoos.

less than successful movies. Others speculated that Semel and Daly were not happy with the diminished role they were expected to play at Time Warner in the 2000s. Nevertheless, when they called it quits, it was the end of a Hollywood era. As Time Warner president Richard Parsons commented in *Time* magazine, "It's kind of like the '98 Yankees. It was a beautiful season. And every season comes to an end."

An unlikely combination

After he left Warner, almost every major studio set its sights on Semel, who was known in the business as a master negotiator. Semel, however, was embracing his newfound freedom. As he told John Greenwald of *Time,* "For the first time in my life I will not have a contract, a road map to follow. This could be the first time I can choose what direction I'm going in." The direction he chose was the Internet, a new medium with untapped potential. Semel launched his own technology investment company called Windsor Media and immersed himself in his newfound field.

When Yahoo went looking for a new CEO in 2001, Semel was not the man who came to most people's minds. The company was established in 1994 by two graduate students, David Filo (1965–) and Jerry Yang (1968–), who were looking for a way to organize the maze of Internet addresses on the World Wide Web. Over the years Yahoo had become a successful provider of Internet and Web-based services, and its owners were millionaires many times over. But with competitors such as Google nipping at their heels, and the bottom dropping out of the computer industry in the late 1990s, Yahoo was feeling the crunch. In January of 2000 Yahoo stock was valued at $235 a share; by mid-2001 it had plummeted to less than $11 per share.

When Semel replaced Tim Koogle as CEO in April of 2001, it may have come as quite a shock to many, but it seemed the logical choice for Jerry Yang. Yang had met Semel in 1997 at an annual media conference in Sun Valley, Idaho. Semel wanted to learn more about the Internet and Yang was impressed by Semel's keen business sense. The two became fast friends, and Semel became something of an unofficial Yahoo advisor. Yang knew that bringing Semel into the fold would cause controversy, but he believed it was worth it. "Everyone talks about what [Semel] did with movies and entertainment," Yang remarked to *Fortune,* "but what he really did was pioneer how to take a piece of content and get it out there. He had a distribution mentality, which at the end of the day is what Yahoo does on the Internet."

Semel did not immediately jump at Yang's offer. He met with company executives and board members, and considered the option carefully. He obviously did not need the money; when he left Time Warner he was a multimillionaire. According to former partner Robert Daly, who spoke with Jim Hu on the CNET News Web site, "Terry was not looking for a job, he was looking for a challenge." Indeed, Semel likened Yahoo to the early challenges he faced at Warner Brothers. As he told Hu, "I think Yahoo has great, strong core assets, and it was those assets that fascinated me and brought me to the table. I love building things and I will look forward to building those assets into a much larger and more diversified company throughout the world."

Yahoo grows up

When the fifty-eight-year-old Semel took the helm of the Sunnyvale, California-based company, he faced a major culture shock. For starters, he was twice as old as the average Yahoo employee. The Yahoo headquarters was something of a giant college campus. A purple cow greeted visitors in the lobby; there was a cubicles-only rule, which meant that all employees from the top down worked in the same equal-sized space; and meetings were usually free-form. The buttoned-down Semel quickly changed the rules. He created his own private office space and he rarely popped in to so say "howdy" to fellow employees the way former CEO Tim Koogle did. Not surprisingly, many employees were suspicious of the non-techie stranger in their midst.

Perhaps their suspicions were well-founded, since Semel lost no time in trimming the ranks. He laid off more than 12 percent of the Yahoo workforce and reduced the number of divisions from forty-four to only four: media and entertainment; communication; premium services; and search. He discontinued the many free-form meetings, where ideas had been launched with no coordination across the company. He created the Product Council, a sort of executive sounding board through which all new ideas had to pass. This ensured that each division head knew about every proposed initiative, and that each initiative was in line with company standards and policies.

During all the changes, Semel took time to learn the lingo. One-hour meetings turned into six-hour marathon sessions, as Semel went over and over the technology terminology. As Jeff Mallett, Yahoo's former president, told *Fortune,* "He'd stay in that conference room for hours until he got it. I think he learned three years of information in six months." So, while he may not have been making great friends in the company, Semel was earning the respect of his colleagues.

Investors say Yahoo

Semel quickly proved that his vision for the company was sound, as he expanded into new areas. When he came on board, 90 percent of

Yahoo's revenues came from on-line advertising, which Semel thought was a shortsighted and rather dangerous way to do business. When the stock market becomes shaky, advertisers tend to pull their advertising, and this greatly contributed to Yahoo's downward spiral in 2000. Semel focused his energies on offering premium services to on-line customers that would require them to pay extra fees. For example, in late 2001 he struck a deal with phone company SBC Communications to offer high-speed Internet access to Yahoo customers.

In addition, Semel made some bold acquisitions. In December of 2001 he launched a takeover of Hotjobs.com, a deal that cost an estimated $436 million, but one that made Yahoo a formidable force in the lucrative world of on-line classifieds. In 2003 Semel positioned Yahoo to take on Google, the monster of all search engines, when he purchased Inktomi and Overture Services, two leaders in the Web search business. Yahoo executives were eager to launch the new Yahoo search engine, a tool that helps on-line users search for information on the World Wide Web, but Semel proceeded with his usual caution. He insisted that company engineers test and retest the system before offering the product to Yahoo customers. He told *Fortune,* "We didn't get into search to do what everyone else is doing. We got into search to change the game."

By mid-2004, only three years after Semel joined Yahoo, the company was in a complete turnaround on all fronts. Its annual revenues doubled from $717 million to $1.4 billion; stock prices rose to more than $40 per share; and for the first time ever, the company appeared on *Fortune* magazine's annual list of the thousand largest corporations in the United States. The new-and-improved Yahoo was attracting 133 million registered users a month, and more than 150,000 advertisers had come on board. Semel the media mogul had become Semel the on-line mastermind, and as *BusinessWeek* proclaimed in late 2003, investors were once again saying "Yahoo!"

For More Information

Books

"David Filo Biography." *Business Leader Profiles for Students.* Vol. 2. Farmington Hills, MI: Gale Group, 2002.

"Jerry Yang Biography." *Business Leader Profiles for Students.* Vol. 2. Farmington Hills, MI: Gale Group, 2002.

Periodicals

Greenwald, John. "Out of the Pictures: Warner Brothers' Legendary Bosses Semel and Daly Exit Time Warner." *Time* (July 26, 1999): pp. 68–69.

Stone, Brad. "Learning the Ropes." *Newsweek* (July 30, 2001): p. 38.

Vogelstein, Fred. "Bringing Up Yahoo." *Fortune* (April 5, 2004): p. 220.

Web sites

Hu, Jim. "Semel: The New Yahoo on the Block." *CNET News.com* (April 17, 2001). http://news.com.com/2100-1023_3-255995.html (accessed on May 28, 2004).

Hu, Jim, and Stephanie Olsen. "Guiding Yahoo from Adolescence to Adulthood." *CNET News.com.* http://news.com.com/1200-1070-959427.html (accessed on May 28, 2004).

"Terry Semel, Yahoo!" *BusinessWeek Online* (September 29, 2003). http://www.businessweek.com/magazine/content/03_39/b3851604.htm (accessed on May 31, 2004).

Yahoo! http://www.yahoo.com (accessed on May 31, 2004).

Nisha Sharma

c. 1982 • India

Activist

In any culture, a cancelled wedding can be a great embarrassment (particularly to the bride), but when Nisha Sharma called off her wedding at the last minute, she not only made front-page headlines in her native India, but became a role model for young women in India and across the world. Shortly before the ceremony, her future husband's family suddenly demanded an illegal dowry payment of $25,000 from her father. An angry Sharma called the police, and the groom was later sentenced to a jail term.

Placed personal ad

Sharma comes from a middle-class Hindu family. She was born in the early 1980s and grew up in Noida, a city near Delhi, which is India's capital. Her father, Dev Dutt, is the owner of a factory that makes car batteries. Sharma was studying computer science when her parents decided to seek a husband for her. In March of 2003 they placed a classified ad in a Delhi English-language newspaper.

Such ads are common in India, where parents arrange marriages for their adult children. Many Indians believe their most important duty as parents is to find worthy spouses for their children, and the honor of the family is often at stake. Sharma and her parents interviewed the candidates who responded to the ad. They were impressed by Munish Dalal, a twenty-five-year-old computer engineer. All parties agreed to the marriage, and the Dalals initially said that no dowry was necessary. Sharma's father, however, gave the Dalals a gift of cash at the engagement party.

The dowry is a centuries-old tradition in India, though it has been prohibited by law since the 1961 Dowry Prohibition Act. It per-

> "My message to all young girls is 'Don't give them a penny.'"

sists in the form of lavish gifts given to the newlyweds and the groom's family by the bride's parents, and sometimes there is cash exchanged. Traditionally, a dowry was the price that the groom's family paid to the bride and her family. It was given because the woman would leave her parents' household and become an income-earner for her in-laws' household instead. The amount was considered compensation for this economic setback.

Dowries persisted into the modern era with a reverse twist: college-educated men with professional jobs are now considered highly eligible spouses, and a woman's parents would offer household goods, including electronics and appliances, to sweeten the deal when they arranged the match. Such items are not called dowry payments, but rather gifts for the newlyweds to start their first home in style. When such gifts are given directly to the bridal couple, they are not considered illegal. Parents often save up for years to be able to afford the items, which can even include real estate and cars. An Indian sociologist, Ashis Nandy, told journalist Ian MacKinnon in the London *Times* that, although the dowry may seem out of place in a modern society like India's, it was "easy money." Nandy commented, "Once

Dowry Prohibition Act of 1961

Nisha Sharma cancelled her own wedding just before it was set to take place, in May of 2003. She called the police, and her father filed a complaint against the groom and his parents for demanding a dowry.

Under India's 1961 Dowry Prohibition Act, gifts or cash given to either the bride or groom by the other's family are illegal if they are made in connection with the marriage. This law was passed to help put an end to the rising number of deaths of young brides at the time. As a widower, the man was then free to marry once again and collect another dowry from another family.

Dowries differ from the "bride-price," and are tied to India's caste system. The caste system placed everyone in a class. The Vaishyas and Shudra castes were obligated to perform only manual-labor jobs. The marriage of a son in such a caste meant that an additional person—his new wife—would be joining the household and bringing in more earnings. Therefore a "bride-price" was paid to the bride's family to compensate for the loss of her labor. In contrast, a dowry was common among the upper castes, the Brahmins and Kshatriyas. The dowries went by the name *sthreedhan,* or woman's share of her parents' wealth. Over the years, this became corrupted into a form of payment made directly to the groom or his family.

Even though India emerged as a modern country with a growing number of educated, profes- sional young people, the dowry endured. Much of the reason for this, critics of the practice have explained, was the high demand for consumer goods among India's growing middle class. Television commercials, for example, show parents giving consumer goods to their overjoyed daughters for their wedding. Such cash or gifts are given to help the newlyweds begin their life together comfortably. Such practices exist in many cultures. In North America wedding showers are held before the ceremony, where invited guests give appliances, dishes, and other household items to the bride and groom, chosen from a gift registry.

In contemporary India, the amount of cash and gifts given is tied to the groom's profession. This comes from the idea that the man's family had spent money to educate him. The higher his professional status, the more eligible a marital prospect he became on the marriage market. In India, young men who work for the country's civil service command the highest price, followed by engineers and doctors.

In India, if such gifts are given without being demanded or tied to the actual wedding vows, then they are not considered illegal. In Sharma's case, however, her fiancé's family asked for an additional $25,000 in cash just before the ceremony began. Munish Dalal and his mother faced up to a ten-year jail sentence and stiff fines for their greed.

Indian families paid to win the bride. Now it's the other way round.... We are left with the belief that women are an economic burden."

Sharma's father had been putting money aside for her wedding-gift package for ten years. He arranged to give the Dalals two of each gift: two televisions, two home-theater sets, two refrigerators, two air

Nisha Sharma, at her home in India, sits in front of boxes of goods bought as her wedding gift. AP/ Wide World Photos. Reproduced by permission.

conditioners, and one car. The second set of goods was for Munish's older brother, who became head of the Dalal household after their father died. "I wanted Nisha to get on well with her in-laws," Dev Dutt told London *Times* journalist Lucy Ash. "I thought it would help if they started off with the same stuff." Vidya Dalal, Sharma's future mother-in-law, went so far as to specify the brands of appliances she wanted.

Groom's mother slapped bride's father

The wedding ceremony was scheduled for a May weekend. Sharma arrived, dressed in the traditional red bridal sari. Her hands and feet were painted with henna, another bridal custom. The guest list was enormous: newspapers reported it as between 1,500 and 2,000 invitees. They waited for the ceremony to begin. Behind the scenes, however, Vidya Dalal asked Sharma's father for a $25,000 cash payment. Dev Dutt recalled in the *Times* interview, "When I said I didn't have that kind of money, Mrs. Dalal asked, 'Well, what have you brought us here for?' and slapped me hard across the face." Their argument erupted into a loud fight, and Mrs. Dalal's sister-in-law spit in Dev Dutt's face, according to the police report.

Sharma learned of the trouble on her way to the ceremony, thanks to a phone call from her brother. When she arrived and found the two families arguing, she was outraged. *People* quoted her as saying, "I thought, 'Has he come to marry me or for the money?'" Knowing the Dalals were breaking the law, she then took the daring step of calling the local police. When they arrived, the police were stunned at what a turn the happy day had taken. They tried to persuade Dev Dutt to let the marriage take place. But Sharma was adamant. "I've never spoken to Dad like that," she told Ash. "Why should anyone else? If they treated him so badly, they probably would have done the same to me, or worse."

Sharma had reason to worry. In India, deaths of young married women were commonplace, and even increasing in number. Some new wives were badly burned in suspicious "kitchen fires." In 2001 alone, there were seven thousand deaths of young women that were linked to their husbands or to members of his family. Experts on domestic violence have claimed that the actual number may even be higher. Such homicides have been tied to resentment over a dowry that is considered too stingy. In other cases, the husband's family demands more goods after the wedding. One women's rights group in India has asserted that three to five women are brought to Indian hospitals every day with suspicious burns. In Delhi, where Sharma lived, there were 130 deaths of young married women in 2002.

The Dalals and their guests fled the wedding ceremony. Sharma's side, however, stayed on through the night to show their support for Sharma and her family. Dev Dutt went to the local police station and made a formal complaint. News organizations learned of this, and Sharma's cancelled wedding made headlines across India the next day. Thanks to the media coverage, the police went to arrest Munish in the early morning hours. His mother was later arrested as well.

Sharma was praised as a hero, an icon, and as the symbol for a new generation of modern Indian women. Women's-rights organizations were quick to defend her actions, and newspapers and other media outlets commended her courage. "It Takes Guts to Send Your Groom Packing," noted one *Times of India* headline, according to a *New York Times* report. The cancellation of a wedding was no minor incident, according to Sanjeev Srivastava, the Delhi correspondent for the *BBC News*. "Especially when the circumstances are as dramatic as the bridegroom's party being sent away," reported Srivastava. "It is always the bride's family which faces ridicule and is looked down upon."

There were no regrets about her decision, Sharma asserted in the numerous interviews she gave to the press in the days afterward. "I'm not remorseful at all," Sharma she told MacKinnon. "It was the right decision. As Munish was leaving the wedding garden he told people he didn't even like me. He was only marrying me for the money and would have thrown me off a balcony in three or four weeks." She was also grateful to her father for taking her side in the matter. Dev Dutt said that he had done so out of concern for her safety. "People say now it will be very difficult to marry my daughter again," Dev Dutt told *New York Times* writer James Brooke. "But I thought, if trouble is starting today, tomorrow may be worse. It could be killing. I thought, let the money go."

Scorned groom spread rumors

Dalal and his mother were also interviewed. They claimed that Sharma had had an affair with another man, and hinted that she showed symptoms of venereal disease. But Sharma's family said that the Dalals had lied on many occasions. Munish had said he was a computer engineer, when he was only a computer instructor—a job with far less status. Sharma' family also claimed that Dalal's mother had said she was the vice principal of a school, when in reality she was only a physical education instructor.

Sharma's cancelled wedding remained one of the top stories in India for days. Several more women followed her example that month, calling off weddings at the last minute and reporting the grooms to the police after financial demands on the women's families had been made. Newspaper stories also noted that Sharma had immediately received marriage proposals from other young men because of her new celebrity status. She was offered a part in a film, and there was even talk of a comic book series that would feature her as an action hero. Six months later she married a computer hardware engineer. There was no elaborate wedding with hundreds of guests this time, just a few dozen invitees. There was also no dowry. Sharma hoped that her actions would inspire other young women. "I can only call on every Indian girl to refuse to give dowry," *Asia Africa Intelligence Wire* quoted her as saying. "My experience has strengthened my belief."

For More Information

Periodicals

Ash, Lucy. " Killing in the Name of Dowry." *Times* (London, England) (July 21, 2003): p. 10.

"The Bride Says No: Nisha Sharma Stops Her Wedding—and Becomes a Symbol—over a $25,000 Dowry." *People* (June 23, 2003): p. 65.

Brooke, James. "World Briefing Asia: India: Anti-Dowry Woman Weds." *New York Times* (November 20, 2003): p. A8.

Brooke, James. "Dowry Too High. Lose Bride and Go to Jail." *New York Times* (May 17, 2003).

Jana, Reena. "Arranged Marriages, Minus the Parents." *New York Times* (August 17, 2000).

Kumar, Lalit. " Nisha Sharma Takes Pheras Happily." *Asia Africa Intelligence Wire* (November 21, 2003).

MacKinnon, Ian. "Dowry Bride's Last-Minute Walkout Delights India." *Times* (London, England) (May 16, 2003): p. 19.

"Mumbai needs a Nisha Sharma." *Asia Africa Intelligence Wire* (May 29, 2003).

Web Sites

Amanpour, Christiane. "For Love of Money." *CBSNews.com.* http://www.cbsnews.com/stories/2003/10/03/60minutes/main576466.shtml (accessed on June 11, 2004).

Kak, Smitri. "Common Girl with Uncommon Grit." *Tribune Online Edition.* http://www.tribuneindia.com/2003/20030525/herworld.htm (accessed on date June 27, 2004).

Srivastava, Sanjeev. "Delhi Girls Rebel over Dowries." *BBC News.* http://news.bbc.co.uk/2/hi/south_asia/3040681.stm (accessed on June 11, 2004).

Russell Simmons

October 4, 1957 • *New York New York*

Business executive

Russell Simmons heads an empire built by rap music. As co-founder of the pioneering record label Def Jam in the 1980s, he helped launch the careers of a number of important artists, such as Run-D.M.C. and the Beastie Boys. His empire includes a clothing line and even an energy drink, but it is his social activism that has caused some to say he might one day make an ideal mayor of New York City. Simmons is often described as the man who made black urban culture a part of the mainstream, but *Newsweek*'s Johnnie L. Roberts noted that "in the view of many, he is now emerging as potentially the most credible and effective leader of the post-civil-rights generation."

Neighborhood was on borderline of rough

Russell Simmons was born in 1957 in Jamaica, a part of Queens in outer New York City. He was the second of three sons in his family, and both his parents were graduates of Howard University in Washington, D.C. His father was a teacher who eventually became a professor of black history at Pace University, and his mother worked for the New York City Parks Department as a recreation director.

The Simmons family moved to the Hollis neighborhood of Queens when Simmons was eight years old. Their home was near a corner that was a known meeting place for drug users and their dealers. His older brother, Danny, was pulled in by the scene and became a heroin addict. Russell seemed headed down a similarly sad road. He began selling marijuana while still in middle school, and for a time was a member of a local gang called the Seven Immortals. When he

> **"Black culture or urban culture is for all people who buy into it and not just for black people. Whether it's film or TV or records or advertising or clothing, I don't accept the box that they put me in."**

was sixteen, he shot at someone who tried to rob him. He was arrested twice on other charges and received a term of probation. Danny, however, wound up serving a stint in jail for drug use.

In 1975, when he was eighteen, Simmons began taking classes at Manhattan City College. He found a job at an Orange Julius outlet in Greenwich Village, but at some point he also financed his club-going lifestyle by selling fake cocaine. If he was caught by the police, he reasoned, he was not doing anything illegal, but Simmons of course faced a bigger threat from angry customers. During these years he hung out at the dance clubs of New York's outer boroughs, where the music was predominantly disco. But then a new movement filtered in, one that had come out of the roughest Bronx and Harlem neighborhoods: performers sang their own rhymes over a classic track, such as "Flashlight" from George Clinton (1941–). Simmons was at one such club in 1977 when he saw how wild the crowd went

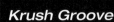
Krush Groove

The 1985 film *Krush Groove* was loosely based on Russell Simmons's life up until that point. It featured an array of top music acts from the era, from Run-D.M.C. and the Beastie Boys to LL Cool J and a young Bobby Brown when he was still a member of New Edition. It was directed by Michael Schultz (1938–), who made two earlier cinematic classics of African American urban life, *Cooley High* and *Car Wash.* Simmons was one of the film's producers.

Two decades after its release, *Krush Groove* has become a cult classic, a snapshot of the early days of rap music when cultural critics and record company executives predicted the style was simply a fad. A then-unknown actor named Blair Underwood (1964–) was cast in the role of New York City music promoter Russell Walker, owner of the label Krush Groove. One of his acts has a surefire hit, but Walker does not have the funds to press the records, and enters into a dangerous financial arrangement with local drug dealers and loan sharks. He also battles with one of his stars over another artist, Sheila E. (1957–), whom both want to date. The plot of the movie, however, was beside the point: Simmons wanted to showcase the array of young talent emerging from New York's black music scene, and depict its vibrancy, too.

over one song from an early rapper and DJ named Eddie Cheeba, and he decided that this was the sound of the future.

His future, in particular. Simmons quit the fake drug business, and eventually left City College just a few credits short of a degree in sociology. He began promoting concerts, and then formed his own management company for artists, which he called Rush Management, after his childhood nickname. Some of the first rap songs ever played on radio were from his acts, including "Christmas Rappin'" from Kurtis Blow (1959–). He also managed Whodini, but it was the group that his teenaged brother, Joey (1964–), joined back in Hollis that put Simmons and his company on the map.

Launched rap's first serious label

Joey was the "Run" in Run-D.M.C., which had a spare, hardcore style of rapping that was also full of clever humor and incisive social commentary. The group's first single, "It's Like That," was released in 1983 and set the tone for the rest of the decade. Simmons helped make his brother's group immensely successful, especially after he teamed with a white college student from Long Island, Rick Rubin (1963–), to launch Def Jam Records in 1985. With their first office

located in Rubin's dormitory room at New York University, they emerged as the first big players on the rap music scene. The label's first single was from LL Cool J (1968–), "I Need A Beat," and helped bring Simmons and Rubin a distribution deal with CBS Records.

During the mid-1980s Simmons became known for his sharp ear and ability to predict the next big thing in music. He helped bring the Beastie Boys to a wider audience, and even revived the careers of the fading rock act Aerosmith, when Run-D.M.C. covered their 1975 hit "Walk This Way." The two groups even made a video together, which became a classic of MTV's first decade on the air. As *Fast Company* writer Jennifer Reingold explained, by 2003 "the marriage of hard rock and rap seems natural, two strands of the same teenage angst and anger. But in the mid-1980s, the idea that black street kids and white suburbanites could like the same music was shocking."

Simmons went on to shepherd such performers as Will Smith (1968–), when he was still the rapper known as "Fresh Prince," as well as Public Enemy, to mainstream success. When asked by model/writer Veronica Webb in an article in *Interview* whether he had "invented" the rap genre, he said no. "I didn't invent it," he explained, "but I was the first to believe that the artist was bigger than the song. Other labels believed that artists only live record to record. I didn't have that disco mentality that you threw the artists away after the song hit." He and Rubin dissolved their business partnership in the late 1980s, but Simmons moved on to conquer audiences elsewhere. He launched Def Comedy Jam, which introduced comedians like Martin Lawrence (1965–) and Bernie Mac (1958–) in the early 1990s, and it became one of the top-rated shows on HBO. In 1992 Simmons founded Phat Fashions, a clothing line, which began growing at a rate of about thirty percent annually over the next decade.

Expanded empire to serve community

Rush Communications became the umbrella group for all of Simmons's ventures. At one point early in the 2000s, these included an energy soda called DefCon3, a wireless phone he designed for Motorola that sold for $549, a joint venture with a top Manhattan advertising agency, a sneaker company with his brother, and the Rush Card, a prepaid Visa debit card aimed at the forty-five million Americans who do not have checking account or access to credit cards.

Simmons said the idea for the debit card came after someone suggested the idea of a prepaid phone card. While the pitch he heard sounded profitable, it was also a rip-off for the users. "I will turn away a deal.... Because people have dollar signs in their eyes," he told *Business Week Online* writer David Liss. "Making money is a pedestrian activity. The challenge is in creating a product or service that the world really needs."

As committed as he is to building an empire that keeps him at the top of the lists of black-owned entertainment companies in America, Simmons is also interested in moving forward on several new fronts. He launched the Def Poetry Jam, which was also carried by HBO and even became a Tony-Award-winning Broadway show in 2003, and he serves as board chair of the Hip-Hop Summit Action Network. The summits are held in various American cities, and mayors regularly appear along with special guests like Snoop Dogg

From left, rapper Eminem, Russell Simmons, Detroit mayor Kwame Kilpatrick, and Dr. Benjamin Chavis, CEO of the Hip-Hop Summitt, backstage at the 2003 Detroit Hip-Hop Summitt. AP/Wide World Photos. Reproduced by permission.

(1972–). They aim to raise political awareness among young Americans, and also serve as a voter registration event. The political power that Simmons was suddenly holding brought all the major presidential hopefuls of the Democratic Party—from John Kerry (1943–) to Al Sharpton (1954–)—to his summit to discuss issues late in 2003.

Devotee of yoga and Deepak Chopra

Simmons sold his remaining stake in Def Jam in 1999 for $120 million. Four years later, his empire was estimated to be bringing in sales of $530 million annually. Much of that came from his clothing line, which he expanded with his wife, former model Kimora Lee Simmons (1975–), to include Baby Phat and Phat Farm Kids. They sold a stake in their company in early 2004 for $140 million, in an attempt to bring it into more department and specialty stores. "When I started," he told *New York* writer Vanessa Grigoriadis in 1998, "they wanted to put me in the ethnic part of the department store. But Phat Farm's best-selling item is a pink golf sweater—it's not a grass skirt or a dashiki." Since then, Simmons has made Phat Farm competitive with such clothing lines as Polo Ralph Lauren and Tommy Hilfiger.

In his 2002 autobiography, *Life and Def: Sex, Drugs, Money and God,* Simmons recounts his business successes and the personal philosophies that keep him grounded. A vegan, he practices yoga daily and makes all his employees read *The Seven Spiritual Laws of Success* by Deepak Chopra (1946–) and then submit a report on the book. Some of his top executives began as interns at the company long ago. "I surround myself with people that share the same spirituality that I believe in," he told Liss. "People who are focused on living better and not just on being out for themselves. I want to be around people who aren't just money-oriented but are focused on how they can give back to the community."

Simmons enjoys a lifestyle that mirrors that of the most successful of his music legends, but it is also one that puts him in the same categories as corporate New York's biggest players. He has an office on the forty-third floor of a midtown Manhattan skyscraper, spends summer vacations in the Hamptons, and lives with his wife and two young daughters in a 35,000-square-foot mansion in Saddle River, New Jersey. He and his wife hosted a fundraiser for Hillary

Clinton (1947–) during her successful bid for a New York State Senate seat in 2002, and he has also worked to overturn the harsh New York State statutes known as the Rockefeller drug laws. These date back to 1973 and the term of Governor Nelson Rockefeller (1908–1979), and force courts to give even first-time drug users long jail terms. Simmons has met with New York Governor George E. Pataki (1945–), and has traveled often to the state capital in Albany to convince legislators to replace these laws with more balanced sentencing guidelines.

Governor Pataki is just one of many high-profile New Yorkers who respect Simmons. According to *Newsweek*'s Roberts, fellow rap mogul Sean "P. Diddy" Combs (1971–) said that "Russell is raising the bar for us with our power to be responsible, not just for ourselves but for our people." Real estate mogul Donald Trump (1946–) told Reingold that "I consider him one of the great entrepreneurs out there today. He's a fabulous guy with a tremendous understanding of business."

Simmons is sometimes mentioned as a future New York mayoral candidate, but he claims to have no political ambitions—other than using his platform to raise awareness about timely issues. These range from the war in Iraq to the New York City school budget. "I'm not telling people anything that's a shock," he said in an *Inc.* interview with Rod Kurtz. "Maybe I'm telling them things they've already heard before. But maybe because of my luck and success, they believe me."

For More Information

Periodicals

Berfield, Susan. "The CEO of Hip Hop; Impresario Russell Simmons Has Brought Urban Style to Mainstream America—And Helped Other Big Marketers Do The Same. An Inside Look at His Growing Influence." *Business Week* (October 27, 2003): p. 90.

Espinoza, Galina. "Phat Cats: Russell and Kimora Simmons Are a Volatile Duo—But They're Coolly Confident about Phat Fashions, Their Hot Hip-Hop Clothing Empire." *People* (July 1, 2002): p. 97.

Greenberg, Julee. "Keeping It Real." *WWD* (April 10, 2003): p. 6.

Grigoriadis, Vanessa. "Russell Simmons: Hip-Hop Honcho." *New York* (April 6, 1998). This article can also be found online at http://www.newyorkmetro.com.

Kurtz, Rod. "Russell Simmons." *Inc.* (April 1, 2004).

Lewis, Miles Marshall. "Russell Simmons's Rap." *Nation* (January 13, 2003): p. 21.

Liss, David. "Tapping the Spirit of Success; Entrepreneur Russell Simmons Thanks Yoga's Philosophy for Giving Him the Principles to Operate His Ever-Growing Hip-Hop Empire." *Business Week Online* (January 13, 2004).

Reingold, Jennifer. "Rush Hour." *Fast Company* (November 2003): p. 76.

Reynolds, J. R. "Rapping with Russell: A Q&A with the CEO." *Billboard* (November 4, 1995): p. 32.

Roberts, Johnnie L. "Beyond Definition: Through His Def Jam Record Label, Russell Simmons Made Hip-Hop into an Unstoppable Cultural Force. Now He's Turning up the Volume in Politics and Business." *Newsweek* (July 28, 2003): p. 40.

Roberts, Johnnie L. "Mr. Rap Goes to Washington: Russell Simmons Helped Take Hip-Hop Mainstream. Can He Make Politics Cool?" *Newsweek* (September 4, 2000): p. 22.

Schlosser, Julie. "Russell Simmons Wants You—To Vote." *Fortune* (May 17, 2004): p. 41.

Webb, Veronica. "Happy Birthday to 'Huge Hefner.'" *Interview* (November 1995): p. 72.

Jessica Simpson

July 10, 1980 • Richardson, Texas

Singer

Pop star Jessica Simpson's career has been something of a roller coaster ride, rife with stomach-lurching highs and lows and unexpected turns. She began singing Christian music professionally as a pre-teen and earned a record deal in her early teens. After several disappointments, she made the transition to pop music. Her star never quite reached the heights that Britney Spears achieved—not until she and husband Nick Lachey appeared in their own reality television series, *Newlyweds.* Then Simpson's career took off with the release of her most successful album to date, *In This Skin,* the launch of her own line of beauty products, and a sitcom in the works.

Sang in church

Jessica Simpson was born on July 10, 1980, in Richardson Texas, north of Dallas. Her father, Joe, was a psychologist and a youth minister. Simpson's first singing experiences were in the church choir. Her talent was evident at an early age and she had begun performing publicly on the gospel circuit by age eleven. When the budding performer found out in 1992 that the Disney Channel was holding auditions for the *New Mickey Mouse Club,* she jumped at the opportunity. Simpson tried out at a regional audition in Dallas and was selected out of more than thirty thousand other contestants as a finalist for a cast position. She lost out to Britney Spears (1981–) and Christina Aguilera (1980–). Although she was disappointed, Simpson's close-knit family encouraged her not to give up on her dream of becoming a singer.

Simpson persisted and a year later, at age thirteen, she was discovered while singing at church camp. The camp's guest speaker, who

> **"I'm such a sucker for big sappy songs. I'm a big romantic and I love love. I love singing about it and listening to songs about it."**

was in the process of launching a record label, saw her belting out an a cappella version of "Amazing Grace." He quickly signed her to the fledgling gospel label, Proclaim Records, and Simpson began working on her first album, *Jessica.* But once the album was completed, Proclaim Records folded, leaving Simpson with a record but no one to sell it. Once again her family urged her to keep fighting for her dream, and Simpson's grandmother put up the money she needed to release *Jessica* herself. To promote the album, Simpson and her father hit the Christian music circuit. Joe Simpson would preach to young adults and Jessica would be the featured musical performer. Afterward, Jessica would sell her CD to moved listeners. Simpson became popular on the circuit and proceeded to open for such well-known spiritual performers as CeCe Winans and Kirk Franklin.

Simpson also took her album to several other Christian record companies, but was turned away again and again. The primary reason for her rejection was her beauty and curvy figure. "They said it could cause guys to lust," Simpson explained to the Knight/Ridder Tribune

Ashlee Simpson

Ashlee Simpson may be following in her older sister's footsteps, releasing a record and starring in her own reality television show, but she is paving her own road to success. While Jessica Simpson has made a name for herself with several pop albums, Ashlee prefers rock music and cites such influences as Janis Joplin (1943–1970) and Chrissie Hynde (1951–). Jessica, who performed on VH1's *Divas Live* in 2004, is the glamorous sister, with her long, blond hair in waves. Ashlee's style is more punk; she frequently wears jeans and lets her hair—dyed brunette—hang straight and loose.

Ashlee Nicole Simpson was born on October 3, 1984, in Texas. She began taking dance lessons at age three. At age eleven, Ashlee was the youngest person ever admitted to the prestigious School of American Ballet. The Simpson family moved to Los Angeles when Ashlee was 14, and she performed with her sister as a background dancer. She then began to pursue an acting career, winning a guest appearance on *Malcolm in the Middle*. In 2002 Simpson earned a regular role on the WB's *7th Heaven,* playing Cecilia Smith for two years.

Simpson's first musical break came in 2003 when her song "Just Let Me Cry" was selected for the soundtrack of *Freaky Friday.* She then signed a record deal with Geffen Records and began work on her debut album. MTV cameras followed Simpson as she met with record executives, co-wrote songs, and recorded tracks. The resulting series, *The Ashlee Simpson Show,* aired in June of 2004. Viewers watched as Simpson went through the process of trying to find the right producers and the right focus for her album, which she hoped to make a reflection of herself and not her famous sister. "[Jessica] is an amazing artist with a beautiful voice," Ashlee told Chuck Taylor of *Billboard.* "But I have never listened to the kind of music that she does. We're both doing music—but in very different ways, and it's cool." The junior Simpson's debut album, *Autobiography,* was released in 2004.

News Service. "…I didn't understand why they were passing judgment on me, especially since I walked in in overalls, nothing revealing."

Unable to obtain a record deal in Christian music, Simpson decided to branch out into pop music. In order to help their daughter make this transition, the Simpson family hired entertainment attorney Tim Medlebaum, who proceeded to set up meetings with nine record labels. When she met with and sang for Sony Music executive Tommy Motolla, he signed her on the spot. Now, with the backing of a major label, Simpson was ready to record her pop debut.

Released debut pop album

Sweet Kisses was released in 1999. The album contained catchy ballads and pop tunes, all emphasized by the singer's expressive vocal ability.

Jessica Simpson performs at VH1 Divas concert, April 18, 2004. Kevin Mazur/WireImage.com.

The album climbed the charts and eventually reached platinum status. The same year Simpson also recorded "Did You Ever Love Somebody" for the soundtrack to the popular television show *Dawson's Creek*. Simpson, well on her way to becoming a major star, toured to promote her album, opening for well-known artists such as Latin pop star Ricky Martin and boy band 98 Degrees. "It was an amazing time for me," Simpson commented on her Web Site. "I was 17 and seeing the world, doing what I loved and doing it in a way that felt right." Simpson also began dating Nick Lachey (1973–), a member of 98 Degrees.

Simpson shortly found herself a major player in the teen pop arena, sharing chart space and magazine covers with other female hit makers including Britney Spears, Christina Aguilera, and Mandy Moore (1984–). The Texas-born vocalist was able to distinguish herself by both exercising her talent and presenting a sexy, though wholesome image. "My whole thing is that I think innocence is sexy. That's my image—that you can be sexy and innocent," Simpson told Ray Rogers in *Interview*. Simpson was an advocate for premarital abstinence and worked hard to be a positive role model for teen girls. In 2000 she turned down the lead in the film *Coyote Ugly* because a particular sex-inclusive scene conflicted with her values.

In 2001, Simpson released her sophomore effort, *Irresistible,* which was a more sophisticated record that reflected the singer's maturity. "This record is about who I am now," she told *Cosmopolitan*. "The music is edgier, and I'm all gown up." Now twenty-one years old, Simpson had learned who she was as a person and an artist. This album, however, did not fare as well commercially as *Sweet Kisses*.

Branching out into acting, Simpson made a guest appearance on *That '70s Show* in 2002, reprising this role twice more in 2003. She also appeared in an episode of *The Twilight Zone*. She then took on a role that would bring her both personal happiness and professional success: the role of wife. Although she and Lachey had broken up for a period of six months in 2001, in part because Simpson, who was eighteen when she began dating Lachey, needed some time on her own to learn who she was independent of a relationship. But the pair soon realized that they belonged together. On October 26, 2002, the two were married. MTV chronicled their lives as a newly married couple with *Newlyweds: Nick and Jessica,* which debuted in August of 2003. The reality show became a huge hit, with 2.7 million viewers tuning in each week. "Going into the show, we both were very clear to each other that we wanted it to be raw and natural and we weren't going to be afraid to fight," Lachey told *Entertainment Weekly.* And so, in addition to the adjustments that came with married life, the couple also had to adjust to the presence of cameras. But they soon got used to the cameras. "We don't have anything to hide.… We wanted people to know how normal we are—that we get frustrated dealing with newlywed things," Simpson told *Redbook*.

Chicken or fish?

Their normalcy is part of what attracted viewers to the show. Simpson and Lachey argued over bills and housekeeping chores, went on a camping trip together, and adjusted to living with each other. As Lachey told *Redbook,* "It's an adjustment getting used to the things she does and her getting used to things that I do. She's sloppier than I would like. She leaves towels lying around and doesn't turn off lights.... It's about finding a middle ground." Viewers have also enjoyed the comic moments of their lives, especially the more ditzy comments that Simpson has made. Her most infamous "dumb blond" moment occurred when, after opening a can of Chicken of the Sea brand tuna, she wondered if she was eating chicken or tuna.

Now a television star, Simpson released her third album, *In This Skin.* The song "With You" was the fastest-rising single of her career. Fans of *Newlyweds* particularly enjoyed her sense of humor about her image, as demonstrated in the music video for "With You," which featured Simpson eating tuna fish. "It's okay to stick your foot in your mouth," she told *Entertainment Weekly,* "just laugh at yourself with everybody else." An expanded version of *In This Skin* was released in the summer of 2004 and included footage from *Newlyweds.* Simpson then went on tour to support her new album.

Building on the success of *Newlyweds* (a second season aired in January of 2004), after her concert tour Simpson tackled several other projects. ABC tapped Simpson and Lachey for the *Nick & Jessica Variety Hour,* which aired in April of 2004. Also in April, Simpson launched a line of kissable, tasteable beauty products, called Dessert Beauty. She also had a sitcom in the works, and was being considered for several movie roles. Simpson has persevered through early career disappointments to achieve her dream of becoming a professional singer, and has surpassed that dream, achieving stardom as a television personality. "I think my definition of true success is success within myself," Simpson told Lance Bass in *Interview.* "People can talk about how many albums you're supposed to sell, or what your videos are supposed to look like, but who are they? If I feel confident about what I'm doing, then I feel successful."

For More Information

Books

Contemporary Musicians, volume 34. Gale, 2002.

Periodicals

Armstrong, Jennifer. "Married … With Cameras: MTV's Nick and Jessica
Are Good Singers, but Better Newlyweds—and They're Not Too
Chicken (or Is it Fish?) to Admit It." *Entertainment Weekly* (January
26, 2004).

Bass, Lance. "Jessica Simpson." *Interview* (August 2001).

Dykstra, Katherine. "Jessica & Nick's True Love Story: in an Exclusive
Interview, They Reveal Their Most Heartbreaking Day, the Night that
Sealed Their Love, and the Secret Thing She Does Very Well." *Redbook* (March 2004).

"Despite Sexy Image, Jessica Simpson Stays True to Her Gospel Roots."
Knight/Ridder Tribune News Service (August 27, 2001).

Kizis, Donna. "Jessica Simpson Sizzles." *Cosmopolitan* (June 2001): p. 182.

"Want a Taste …? Jessica Simpson, Randi Shinder Launch Dessert Beauty
First-Ever Kissable, Tasteable Fragrance and Body Care Collection to
Be Unveiled This Month." PR Newswire (April 26, 2004).

Rogers, Ray. "Jessica Simpson." *Interview* (December 1999).

Taylor, Chuck. "Singing's Not an Act for Simpson." *Billboard* (July 17,
2004).

Web Sites

"Ashlee Simpson Biography." *All Music Guide* http://www.allmusic.com/
cg/amg.dll?p=amg&searchlink=ASHLEE|SIMPSON&uid=MIDMR04
08231148&sql=11:z8de4j176wa4~T1 (accessed on August 23, 2004).

"Ashlee Simpson." *Internet Movie Database* http://www.imdb.com/name/
nm1249883 (accessed on August 23, 2004).

Jessica Simpson http://www.jessicasimpson.com (accessed on August 23,
2004).

"Jessica Simpson Biography." *All Music Guide* http://www.allmusic.com/
cg/amg.dll?p=amg&uid=CADMR0408231401&sql=11:rhuf6j377190
~T1 (accessed on August 23, 2004).

Lemony Snicket (Daniel Handler)

1970 • San Francisco, California

Author, poet

Many writers publish their work under a pseudonym, or alternate name. But Daniel Handler, a.k.a. Lemony Snicket, may be the only writer to have three identities. As Catherine Mallette of the *Fort Worth Star-Telegram* explained, Handler is "an author who is simultaneously a fictional character named Snicket, a representative of a fictional character named Snicket, and a best-selling writer." Under his given name, Daniel Handler, he has published two novels for adults, *The Basic Eight* and *Watch Your Mouth*. In addition, he has published eleven of the planned thirteen books in a series for children called *A Series of Unfortunate Events* under the name Lemony Snicket. Snicket, however, continually misses his public appearances, due to some unforeseen disaster, and Handler must step in and inform the masses of children who have come to see Snicket that they will have to settle for Snicket's representative—Handler.

Preferred dark fiction as a youth

Daniel Handler was born in 1970 in San Francisco, California, the son of an accountant and a college dean. An avid reader, he hated books that were overly happy. "If a book had a syrupy ending, he'd toss it aside," Handler's father, Louis, recalled to James Sullivan of *Book*. "It drove him crazy." Instead, Handler preferred darker works by such writers as Roald Dahl (1916–1990) or Edward Gorey (1925–2000). He attended Lowell High School, a prestigious San Francisco school, graduating in 1988. For college, he selected Wesleyan University. He began writing poetry and won the 1990 Poets Prize from the Academy of American Poets. But he soon turned toward the longer form of fic-

> **"What I think has rankled some people about the books is that they show that if you're good, you're not necessarily rewarded."**

tion. After graduating from Wesleyan he won an Olin Fellowship, the funding from which allowed him to write his first novel. Handler spent the mid-1990s working on his novel, and also wrote comedy sketches for a national radio show. He then moved to New York City, where he worked as a freelance book and movie critic.

The Basic Eight was published in 1999. The book takes the form of a diary, written by the character Flannery Culp while she is in prison for the murder of a teacher and fellow high school student. In her journal, she recalls the events of her senior year at Roewer High School that led to the murders. Reviews for Handler's debut novel were mixed. *Publishers Weekly* noted that the author's "confident satire is not only cheeky but packed with downright lovable characters whose youthful misadventures keep the novel neatly balanced between absurdity and poignancy." The *New Yorker,* however, noted that "the book is weakened by his [Handler's] attempt to turn a clever idea into social satire."

Handler's next novel, *Watch Your Mouth,* (2000) was the tale of Joseph, a college junior who lets his studies slide after falling in love.

After finishing one class with a grade of incomplete (given when a student does not complete all the requirements of a class), his girl-friend, Cynthia, whom he calls Cyn, invites him to spend the summer with her family in Pittsburgh. Joseph is delighted at the chance to spend this summer with Cyn. But after he meets her family, a dark suspicion builds in his mind—that Cyn's family is involved in incest. Handler's second effort again received mixed reviews. Some critics praised the quirky quality of the book, while others found the story too twisted for their taste.

Lemony Snicket is born

According to the Lemony Snicket Web site, "Lemony Snicket was born before you were, and is likely to die before you as well." Snicket's birth date may be unclear, but he was first conceived as Handler's first novel was being published. Since the novel was set in a high school, it was sometimes mistakenly sent to editors of children's books. Editor Susan Rich saw real potential for Handler as a children's author and approached him about trying to write for a younger audience. At first Handler was resistant, but he then pitched an idea for the kind of story that he would have enjoyed as a kid: a dark tale about three orphans who have lost their parents in a fire and are sent to live with a distant cousin, Count Olaf, who wants nothing more than to steal the children's inheritance. Handler never expected his idea to receive the publisher's support, but Rich loved it and soon Handler was at work on the first of *A Series of Unfortunate Events*.

The story of the three Baudelaire children—Violet, Klaus, and Sunny—is told by Lemony Snicket, a name Handler first invented in order to keep himself off of unwanted mailing lists. The biography of Snicket on the Lemony Snicket Web site notes that he was born in a country that is now underwater and has been researching the lives of the Baudelaire orphans for "several eras." Snicket is described on the Web site as "eternally pursued and insatiably inquisitive, a hermit and a nomad." Readers who wish to learn more about the life of Lemony Snicket can turn to *Lemony Snicket: The Unauthorized Autobiography*. Published in 2002, the autobiography features thirteen chapters of notes, songs, letters, photos, newspaper clippings, and other documents. The book additionally includes more information about the characters

A Series of Unfortunate Events: The Series

Below are the first eleven books of the planned thirteen in the series.

The Bad Beginning, 1999.

The Reptile Room, 1999.

The Wide Window, 2000.

The Miserable Mill, 2000.

The Austere Academy, 2000.

The Ersatz Elevator, 2001.

The Vile Village, 2001.

The Hostile Hospital, 2001.

The Carniverous Carnival, 2002.

The Slippery Slope, 2003.

The Grim Grotto, 2004.

in *A Series of Unfortunate Events.* The book also suggests that there is a connection between the Snicket family and the Baudelaires. Handler, as Snicket's representative, wrote the preface to the book.

A Series of Unfortunate Events starts with *The Bad Beginning,* published in 1999. On the first page, Snicket lets his readers know what kind of story they are in for: "If you are interested in stories with happy endings," he writes, "you would be better off with another book. In this book, not only is there no happy ending, there is no happy beginning, and very few happy things in the middle." Regardless of the lack of "happy" material, *The Bad Beginning* and each subsequent installment of the series was embraced by readers of all ages. Handler was dumbfounded by the huge success of the Snicket books. "I thought [Susan Rich and I] were two crazy people," he told Mallette. "Then I thought the publishing house was a bunch of crazy people. Now, it seems everyone's crazy. The books just failed to fail." Indeed, by 2003 the books had sold more than thirteen million copies, had been translated into thirty-seven languages, and had been sold in over forty countries.

Success comes as a surprise

Part of the success of the books is due to the fact that Snicket does not talk down to his young readers. He uses big words, and humorously inserts vocabulary lessons. Some readers, however, have objected to Snicket's books. These critics consider them too dark for children and disapprove of the fact that every adult the children meet is, according to Mallette, "completely clueless and incompetent." The books have even been banned in Decatur, Georgia. But Handler argues that the message of the Snicket books is true to life: good behavior is not automatically rewarded, but you should always try to do the right thing anyway. The Baudelaire children must rely on their wits to escape each disaster, rather than expecting that good things will come their way simply because they are good.

A movie based on the first three books in the series was set for release in December of 2004. The film stars Jim Carrey (1962–) as the evil Count Olaf and features Meryl Streep (1949–) as Aunt Josephine. Jude Law (1972–) narrates the film in the role of Snicket. Fans of the books eagerly awaited the film, but the Lemony Snicket Web site warned, "Unless you have a taste for dark rooms, sticky floors, stale popcorn, and unhappy endings, steer clear of the movie."

Lemony Snicket's Inspiration: Edward Gorey

The first book that Daniel Handler bought with his own money was *The Blue Aspic* by Edward Gorey. Born in Chicago in 1925, Gorey was a writer and illustrator who published more than one hundred books. Like Handler's books, Gorey's work appeals to a wide age group. His children's books create a dark world where children are not safe from unhappy events. Alison Lurie, writing in *New York Times Review of Books,* noted that children in Gorey's books "fall victim to natural disasters, are carried off by giant birds, or are eaten by comic monsters…. Yet somehow the overall effect is not tragic but comic."

After graduating from high school, Gorey served in the U.S. Army from 1944 to 1946. He attended Harvard University, earning a degree in French. Gorey then went to work for the publishing company Doubleday in 1953, serving as illustrator for several books. His first book, *The Unstrung Harp,* was also published that year. He later left Doubleday, forming his own independent press. His first children's book was *The Doubtful Guest* (1957), in which a family finds themselves housing a most unusual guest—a creature that looks like a cross between a penguin and an anteater and wears high-top sneakers and a flowing scarf. One of his most notorious children's books, *The Gashlycrumb Tinies,* was published in 1962. This alphabet book chronicles the deaths of twenty-six children, all in rhyming order: "A is for AMY who fell down the stairs / B is for BASIL assaulted by bears."

Although many of his books were intended for children as well as adults, they were not all published as children's books. To this day, critics argue if Gorey's work can be considered children's literature, given the dark subject matter and "unfortunate events" that happen to children in these stories. It is this very belief that children need to be protected from unhappy events that the Lemony Snicket books reject. In addition to writing and illustrating, Gorey also designed sets for theatrical productions, beginning with a 1977 version of *Dracula* for which he received a Tony Award. Gorey, who never married, died of a heart attack in April of 2000.

Daniel Handler is married to Lisa Brown, a graphic artist. The couple has one child. Lemony Snicket dedicates each book to a woman named Beatrice. The details of Beatrice's relationship to Snicket remain a mystery. When asked about Beatrice's identity he responded on the Lemony Snicket Web site, "This answer is so terrible that I cannot even begin to say it without weeping. O Beatrice! My Beatrice!"

For More Information

Books

"Edward Gorey." *Authors and Artists for Young Adults,* Volume 40. Gale Group, 2001.

"Lemony Snicket." *Contemporary Authors Online,* Gale, 2004.

Periodicals

Fierman, Daniel. "Lemony Snicket." *Entertainment Weekly* (April 23, 2004): p. 58.

Lurie, Alison. "On Edward Gorey (1925–2000)." *New York Times Review of Books* (May 25, 2000): p. 20.

Mallette, Catherine. "Tracking Lemony Snicket. The True Story (Well, Mostly) of the Mysterious, Fugitive, Best-Selling Author of A Series of Unfortunate Events." *Fort Worth Star-Telegram* (Fort Worth, Texas) (September 24, 2003).

"Review of *The Basic Eight*." *Publishers Weekly* (March 1, 1999): p. 59.

"Review of *The Basic Eight*." *New Yorker* (June 21, 1999).

Scott, Laura. "Review of *Lemony Snicket: The Unauthorized Autobiograhy*." *School Library Journal* (July 2002): p. 124.

Sullivan, James. "He's Having a Baby: This Halloween, After Four Years of Torturing Children, Superstar Author Lemony Snicket is Getting Exactly What He Deserves." *Book* (November–December 2003).

Web Sites

LemonySnicket.com. http://www.lemonysnicket.com (accessed on August 25, 2004).

Annika Sorenstam

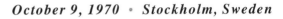

October 9, 1970 • ***Stockholm, Sweden***

Golfer

Swedish golfer Annika Sorenstam is one of the best golfers to set foot on the green. She won the first two U.S. Opens that she competed in and has been inducted into the World Golf Hall of Fame. "I'm very proud about what I've done and pleased about my career," she told *Golf World*. By June of 2004 she had fifty-two victories to her credit, ranking her in sixth place among the best players in golf history. With such impressive achievements behind her, she began to consider the possibility of retiring in the next few years.

Chose golf over tennis

Annika Sorenstam was born on October 9, 1970, in Stockholm, Sweden. Her father, Tom, was an executive for IBM. Both her parents were athletically inclined, and participated in several sports including track and field, handball, basketball, and golf. As a youth Sorenstam most enjoyed playing tennis. She participated in her first tennis tournament at age five, but by age sixteen she began to feel burned out on the sport. She had begun playing golf at age twelve, and now turned her energies toward this sport. Golf, she found, suited her better than tennis. "In tennis, you always have to have a partner.... In golf, I could be on my own," she told *SI.com*. She qualified for the Swedish junior national team, and her career took off from there.

In 1990 Sorenstam was offered an athletic scholarship to the University of Arizona at Tuscon. In her freshman year she won the National Collegiate Athletic Association (NCAA) golf championship and was also named College Player of the Year. She left school after her second year in order to play golf professionally. She went to

> "I am a person that's all or nothing. If I can't be on top, because I have been there, then I don't know if I can handle that. I don't like finishing in the middle. I never have."

Europe, qualifying for the European Women's Tour in 1993. She was named Rookie of the Year on that tour. The following year she qualified for the Ladies Professional Golf Association (LPGA) and earned the title of Rookie of the Year. In 1995 Sorenstam finished in the top ten for seven of the eleven tournaments and then won the U.S. Women's Open, which is the most prestigious event in women's golf. That same year she was awarded the Vare Trophy, given to the player with the lowest scoring average of the season, and was named LPGA Player of the Year.

After working so hard for all her achievements in the early 1990s, Sorenstam needed a break. She gave herself until mid-March of 1996 before returning, refreshed, to the golf circuit. Once again, she won the Women's Open, as well as the Vare Trophy—this time with the second lowest score ever (70.47), next to Beth Daniels who finished 1989 with an average score of 70.38. She also won the Samsung World Championship of Golf and the CoreStates Betsy King

Annika Sorenstam hits from the sand trap during the Bank of America Colonial. AP/Wide World Photos. Reproduced by permission.

Classic. Sorenstam made the top ten in fourteen tournaments and finished in the top five seven times.

Failed to win a three-peat

No women's golfer had ever won at the U.S. Open three times in a row. In 1997 the pressure was on Sorenstam to do just that. Although she performed admirably that year, with six wins—the Chrystler-Plymouth Tournament of Champions, the Cup Noodles Hawaiian Ladies Open, the Longs Drug Challenge, the Michelob Light Classic, the CoreStates Betsy King Classic, and the ITT LPGA Tour Championship—she could not pull off another Women's Open win. Her top rival that year was Kerrie Webb, who took the 1997 Vare Trophy. But the competition inspired Sorenstam to work harder, and she was once more named the LPGA Rolex Player of the Year.

In 1998 Sorenstam reclaimed the Vare Trophy, breaking Beth Daniels' record by finishing the year with an average score under seventy. She won five more championships: the Safeco Classic, the Michelob Light Classic, the ShopTire LPGA Classic, and the JAL Big Apple Classic. The following year she won only one tournament, but in 2000 she performed at top level, winning five championships.

In 2003 Sorenstam became the first woman to play in a Professional Golf Association (PGA) event in fifty-eight years. That May she competed in the Bank of America Colonial. However, not all of her fellow players appreciated her presence. Two weeks before the tournament, Vijay Singh said, according to *SI.com,* "I hope she misses the cut." Although Sorenstam did fail to make the final cut, she found the experience invaluable, feeling that she had come away from the Colonial a better player. She called the event "the greatest thing that will ever happen to me, golfwise," as quoted by Steve Elling of the Knight/Ridder Tribune News Service. "The pressure I was under, I figured if I can handle that, I should be able to handle everything."

Inducted into Hall of Fame

That same year Sorenstam was inducted into the World Gold Hall of Fame, becoming the youngest person ever admitted to the Hall. For her, 2003 was "definitely the most memorable year I've had," according to Elling. Indeed, after winning three of the four major LPGA tournaments and participating at Colonial, 2003 could easily be considered her best season yet.

Yet the Women's Open title still eluded her. After her two initial wins, she failed to claim another U.S. Open title. She had come close several times but, as she told Hank Goal of the Knight/Ridder Tribune News Service, "A lot of the time I get in my own way. I want it so badly that I screw up." But Sorenstam did not let this get her down. "The competition is tough; the courses are tough," she told Gola. "But I've learned a little bit the last few years." Her game-plan for future U.S. Opens was, as she told Gola, "to go back to basics, playing my own game, taking it one day at a time and one shot at a time."

By 2004 Sorenstam had begun to talk about the possibility of retirement. Her desire is to keep playing as long as she still enjoys the game and pushing herself to perform at top level. But, as she told David Teel of the Knight/Ridder Tribune News Service, "The competition is getting tougher every year. So the question is how much longer can I do that? I think that will determine how long I play." Sorenstam married David Esch in January of 1997. In her free time, she enjoys computers, cooking, and music.

For More Information

Books

"Annika Sorenstam." *Great Women in Sports.* Visible Ink Press, 1996.

Periodicals

Elling, Steve. "Sorenstam Makes It to Hall." Knight/Ridder Tribune News Service (October 20, 2003).

Gola, Hank. "Sorenstam Struggling Heading into U.S. Open." Knight/Ridder Tribune News Service (July 2, 2004).

Sirak, Ron. "Let the Debate Begin: As Annika Sorenstam Adds Seventh Major Trophy to Her Collection, Some Peers Ask: Is She the Best Female Golfer Ever?" *Golf World* (June 18, 2004).

Teel, David. "When Sorenstam Exits LPGA, It Will Be on Her Terms." Knight/Ridder Tribune News Service (May 6, 2004).

Web Sites

"Daddy Knows Best: Sorenstam Owes Success to Father's Early Lessons." *SI.com* (October 18, 2003). http://sportsillustrated.cnn.com/2003/golf/10/18/bc.glf.sorenstam.ssucce.ap/index.html (accessed on August 26, 2004).

Gary Soto

April 12, 1952 • Fresno, California

Author

Gary Soto is a man who writes from experience. He grew up in one of the many barrios (poor Mexican American neighborhoods) of Fresno, California, and since the mid-1970s he has borrowed from that community to create an astonishing number of works. Soto, however, does not see himself as strictly a Chicano author. True, in his over twenty books of poetry and prose for adults and in over thirty books for younger readers, he focuses on the daily trials and tribulations of Spanish-speaking Americans. But, through crisp, clear imagery and his true-to-life characters, Soto connects with readers of all ages and backgrounds. As he explained in his Scholastic *Booklist* biography, "Even though I write a lot about life in the barrio, I am really writing about the feelings and experiences of most American kids." As a result, Soto is considered to be one of the most important contemporary authors in the United States.

Life in the barrio

Gary Soto was born on April 12, 1952, the second child of Manuel and Angie Soto. The family lived in Fresno, California, and like many Mexican Americans Soto's parents and grandparents worked as laborers in the surrounding San Joaquin Valley, the agricultural center of the state. Typical jobs included picking oranges, cotton, and grapes for very little pay, or working in the often dangerous packing houses of local businesses, such as the Sunmaid Raisin Company. When Soto was just five years old, his father was killed in an accident while working at Sunmaid. Manuel Soto's death had a devastating effect on his family, both emotionally and economically. Gary was hit particu-

"Of poetry or prose, I prefer poetry as part of my soul. I think like a poet, and behave like a poet."

larly hard and spent years brooding over the accident. And Angie Soto was left with three small children to raise: oldest son Rick, middle child Gary, and Debra, the youngest.

After Manuel Soto's death, the family moved to a rough neighborhood in an industrial area of Fresno. To make ends meet, Angie Soto and the children's grandparents took what jobs they could find. As Gary and his siblings grew older they, too, worked in the fields and factories of Fresno. Regardless, the family struggled. Working left little time for school, and when Soto did go, he made very poor marks. While attending Roosevelt High School, he maintained a D average, and spent more time chasing girls than doing his homework. Soto received little encouragement from home to do better. As he explained in interviews, education was simply not part of their culture—the culture of poverty. "Our shelves were not lined with books," Soto told *Quill* editors, "they were lined with menudo." Menudo is a type of spicy Mexican soup.

Although Soto was not encouraged to read at home, he was exploring the world of books on his own at the school library. Some of his favorites were by American authors such as Ernest Hemingway

United Farm Workers of America

Gary Soto is the Young People Ambassador for the United Farm Workers of America (UFWA), which means that during his many visits to libraries and schools, he introduces kids to the legacy of the United Farm Workers organization. The UFWA is the largest organization of farm workers in the United States. Through bargaining agreements, contract negotiations, and other tactics, its members work to improve the wages and working conditions for all agricultural workers in America. This includes fighting for such basic rights as a living wage, access to clean drinking water and bathrooms, and safe working conditions.

The beginnings of the UFWA can be traced to the 1950s when the *bracero* program was in effect in the United States. Following World War II (1939–45), there was a shortage of field laborers in California and Texas where agriculture was a key industry. As a result, an agreement was made between Mexico and the United States, where U.S. growers were allowed to offer short-term work contracts to Mexicans. Eventually, growers became dependent on these seasonal laborers, who were willing to take on back-breaking work for little pay, work that most Americans were not willing to do. Because they were not citizens of the United States, because they usually spoke little English, and because they were not organized under a union, conditions for Mexican laborers were poor. Their temporary housing often lacked indoor plumbing, and children were often forced to work in the fields in order to help their family survive. By the mid-1960s, there were hundreds of thousands of laborers living and working in such substandard conditions.

In 1966, the National Farm Workers Organizing Committee (UFWOC) was founded by two leaders in the Mexican American community who had been fighting for labor rights for years, Cesar Chávez (1927–1993) and Dolores Huerta (1930–). Their first combined effort involved organizing Chicano and Filipino workers in the California grape-picker strike of 1965–66. After a bitter battle between growers and workers, the UFWOC secured contracts with two of the largest grape growers in California; the contracts included among other things, a promise to ban the use of harmful pesticides, access to washing facilities, and rest periods. This was first successful bargaining agreement between farm laborers and growers in the United States.

Since then the organization has continued to fight for the rights of workers in all types of agricultural industries, from grapes to lettuce, from strawberries to mushrooms. Today, according to the UFWA Web site, farm workers who are employed by companies that accept UFWA contracts enjoy decent pay, family medical care, pensions, and other similar benefits. Unfortunately, the site also reports that the majority of farm laborers in California and the rest of the country still do not enjoy these basic protections. This means that the battle continues, carried on by the next generation.

(1899–1961) and John Steinbeck (1902–1968). Soto was especially inspired by one book in particular, *To Sir with Love,* a novel written by E. R. Braithwaite (1920–) about a teacher who devotes himself to students at a school in the East End working-class district of London, England. Reading that novel prompted Soto to enroll at Fresno City College after graduation. He was not sure exactly what he would study in college, perhaps geography or paleontology (the study of fossils). Soto, however, was sure that he did not want to be a farm worker. And, although he loved to read, the thought of becoming a writer did not even cross his mind.

Poet of the people

But, once again, a chance encounter in the library would change Soto's course. When he was nineteen and in his second year at Fresno College, the young student discovered a collection of contemporary poetry. As Soto remarked to *Quill,* "I thought that poetry had to be about mountains and streams and birds and stuff." But one poet, Edward Field (1924–), was a native of New York and his poems, which were about "trash and smog," hit a chord. As Soto further explained, "Field wrote in a voice that was real common and I didn't know poetry could be like that." After Field, Soto stumbled upon the works of Chilean poet Pablo Neruda (1904–1973). "I was bitten." he commented in a "Between the Lines" interview, "I wanted to do this thing called writing poetry."

Soto transferred to California State University, Fresno, and in 1972 he took his very first poetry-writing class. From 1972 until 1973 he studied with noted Detroit, Michigan, poet Philip Levine (1928–), who was known for his poems about working-class people. Levine taught Soto not only how to take apart and analyze poems, but also about the nuts and bolts of writing his own poetry. In 1974, Soto graduated from Cal State with a bachelor's degree in English. The following year he began working on a master's degree in creative writing at the University of California, Irvine. That same year he married Carolyn Oda, the daughter of Japanese American farmers. The couple has one daughter, Mariko Heidi Soto. In 1977, with master's degree in hand, Soto began teaching Chicano studies at the University of California at Berkeley. He remained at the university until 1993, as an associate professor of both Chicano studies and English.

While still a student, Soto began publishing poems and winning prizes, and in 1977 he released his first book of poetry, called *The Elements of San Joaquin.* Most of the poems paint a bleak picture of Mexican American life in central California, and Soto received widespread praise for his vivid descriptions, which were sometimes disturbing, but always truthful. The young poet was immediately recognized as an emerging talent, and his following books of poetry further cemented his reputation and garnered him a countless number of prizes. In 1978, Soto released his second collection, *The Tale of Sunlight,* which was nominated for a Pulitzer Prize, one of the highest honors in the United States given each year for achievement in journalism or literature. He was one of the first Mexican Americans to be so honored.

Soto the master storyteller

By 1985 Soto had produced four books of poetry and been published in numerous poetry magazines. That same year he branched out and published his first book of prose, called *Living Up the Street: Narrative Recollections.* Considering Soto's poems often had a storytelling feel to them, the jump to prose seemed natural. And, just as in his poetry, Soto mined his childhood memories of life in Fresno to fuel his work. *Living Up the Street,* was followed by three other collections of autobiographical essays: *Small Faces* (1986), *Lesser Evils: Ten Quartets* (1988), and *A Summer Life* (1990). In 2001, several of these essays, along with some new material, were compiled in a single volume called *The Effects of Knut Hamsun on a Fresno Boy.*

In all of his autobiographical works, readers are introduced to Soto's neighborhood through snapshot descriptions of family, friends, sights, sounds, and smells. In fact, Soto was praised for having a seemingly photographic memory of such ordinary things as "my grandmother sipp[ing] coffee and tearing jelly-red sweetness from a footprint-sized Danish" or a jacket that was the "color of day-old guacamole." In a 1988 *BookPage* interview, Soto explained his ability to write with such clarity: he grew up in a blighted area of South Fresno, and "these are the pictures I take with me when I write. They stir up the past, the memories that are so vivid."

Such clear recollections of his youth served Soto well in the 1990s when he turned to writing stories aimed specifically at young readers. Soto claimed, in his *BookList* biography, that he began writing for children because he wanted to "start Chicanos reading." He also wanted to remedy the fact that there were very few books available to young people that featured Mexican Americans. As Rudolfo Anaya remarked in *World Literature Today,* "Entire generations of

Mexican American schoolchildren went through elementary school without ever having read a story about their culture and their communities." Soto set out to change all that in his first collection of stories for children, called *Baseball in April,* published in 1990.

Baseball features a different character in each of the eleven stories, but all are set in poorer districts of central California. In one story a young girl named Yollie laments the fact that she doesn't have a new dress to wear to the eighth-grade dance; in another, two young boys play baseball for the neighborhood Hobo team because they don't make the Little League team for the third year in a row. Although Soto writes the stories in English, he sprinkles Spanish expressions and phrases throughout, a trend he continued in future works. Sometimes he even includes a glossary of Spanish terms to help his non-Spanish speaking readers. And, although the stories have a distinct Latino flavor, they appeal to all types of children. As Diane Roback of *Publisher's Weekly* commented, "The conflicts and feelings expressed are universal."

Famous children's author

Soto was always a very prolific writer, but after he left teaching in 1993, his pace picked up even more. By the mid-1990s, he was producing as many as three children's books per year. In addition, he dabbled in all types of writing for young readers of all ages. There are books of poetry, including *A Fire in My Hands* (1991), *Canto Familiar* (1995), and *Fearless Fernie* (2002); picture books for very young children, such as *Too Many Tamales* (1992), *If the Shoe Fits* (2002), and the Chato the Cat tales; as well as chapter books for kids in middle school, which include *The Skirt* (1992), *The Pool Party* (1993), and *Boys at Work* (1995). Soto also writes young adult novels aimed at older teens. As Susan Marie Swanson wrote in a *Riverbank Review* profile, "A child could grow up on Soto's books."

Soto's poetry for children is much lighter in tone than his adult works; as he does in his autobiographical prose, he celebrates small moments from his childhood that can be understood by any young person growing up anywhere. For example, he writes about such everyday activities as running through a lawn sprinkler on a sunny, summer afternoon, going on a first date, or feeding the birds. Some of his middle school novels, such as *Summer on Wheels* (1995) are also lighter fare and show off the silly, quirky side of Soto. On the other hand, several of Soto's novels are hard-hitting, with characters facing some very tough issues. In *Taking Sides* (1991), for example, eighth-grader Lincoln Mendoza moves from his inner-city neighborhood to a suburb of Fresno that is predominantly Anglo, or white; as a result his loyalties for his old friends are challenged.

When Soto writes for older teens, the topics can be quite complex. One example is the novel *Jesse* (1994), which the author claims is his personal favorite, perhaps because, as Soto has revealed, it is the most autobiographical. The story takes place in the early 1960s and is set against the turbulent backdrop of the Vietnam War (1954–75) protests and the beginning of the United Farm Workers movement, an organization that was established to fight for the rights of farm laborers in California. Sixteen-year-old Jesse leaves home to escape an abusive father, but when he moves in with his older brother he ends up facing a host of other problems, including racism both at his new school and at work.

Soto further explores the pressure of growing up as a young Mexican American in 1997's *Buried Onions,* which chronicles the story of Eddie, a young man struggling to escape poverty and gang life by going to school and staying far away from his *cholos,* his gang friends. Soto picks up the story of gang life in the novel's sequel, *The Afterlife,* published in 2003. But, whereas *Buried Onions* was described by critics as bleak, *Afterlife,* was considered to be "filled with hope." An ironic comment, considering the main character, seventeen-year-old Chuy, is tragically killed on page two of the book by a knife-wielding stranger. In death, however, Chuy is given the opportunity to explore his life. The story is told from his ghostly perspective, as he roams the streets of the Fresno barrios and visits friends who mourn his passing and family members who seek to avenge his death. As Chuy's ghostly body begins to disappear, he realizes that his life, no matter how brief, was worth living.

Connects with readers

By the mid-2000s, Soto gave no indication that he was slowing down. He continued to publish books for both adults and children, and when not pursuing other interests such as reading, traveling, or gardening, he was at his desk writing for at least four to five hours per day. Soto also spent a good deal of time on the road, visiting schools and libraries in order to connect with fans of his books and would-be readers. In his *Booklist* biography, he describes playing basketball and baseball with young people who come to his readings, singing songs with them, and even acting in skits. "I do these things because I want to make sure kids get excited about reading," Soto explained.

In 2004 plans were in the works to make *Buried Onions* into a movie, with an expected release date of late 2005. As a result, publishers expect sales of Soto's books to soar even more. When asked by *Quill* why his books have such a universal appeal considering most focus on the specific community of Fresno, California, Soto replied: "I think we are all the same. We might change in dress, we might change in dance or music, we might change in skateboarding or little things like that. But basically, we have the same motive. We like to eat, we like to love, we like to enjoy our free time and friendship. Those things don't change, no matter what."

For More Information

Books

"Gary Soto." *Major Authors and Illustrators for Children and Young Adults.* 2nd ed. Farmington Hills, MI: Gale Group, 2002.

Periodicals

Roback, Diane. "Review of *Baseball in April*." *Publisher's Weekly* (March 30, 1990): p. 64.

Swanson, Susan Marie. "Gary Soto." *Riverbank Review* (Fall 1999): pp. 16–18.

Web Sites

Anaya, Rudolfo. "Gary Soto of the United States." *World Literature Today* (November 2002) http://www.ou.edu/worldlit/NSK/Soto.htm (accessed on August 10, 2004).

"Gary Soto Biography." *Scholastic Books: Author Studies Homepage.* http://www2.scholastic.com/teachers/authorsandbooks/authorstudies/authorhome.jhtml?authorID=89&collateralID=5285&displayName=Biography (accessed on August 10, 2004).

Gary Soto Web site. http://www.garysoto.com/ (accessed on August 10, 2004).

Pham, Thy and Camile Orillaneda. "Interview with Gary Soto." (May 7, 2003) *Quill Web site* http://mpnet.esuhsd.org/quill 2003/132.pdf (accessed on August 10, 2004).

Soto, Gary. "Between the Lines: Interview with Gary Soto." (September 2003) *Harcourt Trade Publishing Web site* http://www.harcourtbooks.com/authorinterviews/bookinterview_Soto.asp (accessed on August 10, 2004).

United Farm Workers of America, AFL-CIO Web site. http://www.ufw.org/ (accessed on August 11, 2004).

Wilson, Etta. "Gary Soto: A Mexican-American Voice that Speaks for All." (May 1988) *BookPage Web site* http://www.bookpage.com/9805bp/gary_soto.html (accessed on August 10, 2004).

Ben Stiller and Owen Wilson

Ben Stiller

November 30, 1965 • *New York City, New York*

Actor, director, writer, producer

Owen Wilson

November 18, 1968 • *Dallas, Texas*

Actor, director, writer

Ben Stiller and Owen Wilson are considered to be one of the top comic duos of the 2000s. But, they are also compared to such legendary comedians as Bud Abbott (1900–1974) and Lou Costello (1906–1959), who appeared as Abbott and Costello in a bevy of films in the 1940s. As Joel Stein of *Time* remarked, "Stiller updates Lou Costello with an agitated everyman quality, while Wilson does the smartest dumb guy ever." The pair has appeared together in six films, including *The Royal Tenenbaums, Zoolander,* and *Starsky & Hutch,* and if they have their say, their run will continue indefinitely. As Stiller told Shaun Adler of *Cinema Confidential,* "We just enjoy each other's company and have fun working together. As long as people seem to allow us to work together, I think it will kinda keep going."

Comedy in the genes

Ben Stiller was born on November 30, 1965, in New York City to legendary comedians Jerry Stiller (c. 1927–) and Anne Meara (1929–). As a comedy team the couple often performed on the popular 1960s variety program *The Ed Sullivan Show.* Meara went on to star in her own short-lived TV series *Kate McShane*; she was also regularly featured on such 1970s sitcoms as *Rhoda* and *Archie Bunker's Place.* To modern audiences, Jerry Stiller is probably best known for his role as Frank Costanza on *Seinfeld.* Because of his parents' work, Ben and older sister Amy basically grew up in show business. They hobnobbed with celebrities and they frequently traveled to set locations, which Stiller enjoyed far more than staying home and hanging out with kids his own age.

When he was very young it was obvious that Stiller would someday follow in his famous family's footsteps. He and his sister

> **"I don't think it's very easy to be funny. I'm just not a naturally cheery person."**
>
> Ben Stiller, *Interview*, April 1996.

regularly wrote and performed their own skits. They also put on plays based on scenes from Shakespeare, which meant that Ben had to wear his sister's tights. In addition, Stiller showed an early knack for directing. At age ten, he began shooting films using a Super-8 camera. The plots of his movies usually followed the same storyline: a bully would pick on young Stiller and he would seek a swift and awful means of revenge. When he was eight years old, the budding actor/director made his first television appearance, playing the violin on *The Mike Douglas Show.* Just two years later, when he was ten, Stiller landed a guest spot on his mother's TV series.

In 1983, after graduating from the Calhoun School in New York, Stiller headed west to attend the School of Theater, Film, and Television at the University of California, Los Angeles. He lasted only nine months. Eager to be out of the classroom and working in show business, Stiller returned to New York where he cut his teeth in theater. He worked as a busboy and waiter until 1986 when he won a small role in the Broadway play *The House of Blue Leaves.* The play featured veteran actor John Mahoney (1940–), who would later costar as Martin

Crane in the long-running sitcom *Frasier.* During production, Stiller collaborated with Mahoney on a short film spoof of the 1986 drama *The Color of Money,* which is about an up-and-coming young pool shark and his older mentor. In Stiller's send-up, he and Mahoney play two conmen who instead of frequenting pool halls, go to bowling alleys and hustle lunch money from school kids.

A show of his own

In the late 1980s, Stiller made some guest appearances on TV; he also made his big screen debut in 1987 in *Empire of the Sun.* In 1989, however, he got his first real break when his *Money* spoof was purchased by Lorne Michaels (1944–), longtime producer of the late-night comedy program *Saturday Night Live* (SNL). Michaels also hired Stiller to join the show as a writer and cast member. Stiller, however, was not happy at SNL, primarily because he was not allowed the freedom to create his own short films. After less than one season he quit the show and headed to Los Angeles where he was hired by MTV. At first, Stiller directed a comedy program called *Colin Quinn: Back to Brooklyn,* but MTV executives were so impressed they pulled Stiller off the show to develop a series of his own.

The Ben Stiller Show debuted on MTV in 1990 and was, as Josh Wolk of *Entertainment Weekly* called it, a "pastiche of pointed pop-culture satire." It aired only briefly, but was picked up by Fox Network in 1992. The half-hour sketch comedy featured Stiller and cast mates doing parodies of everything from infomercials to bad 1970s TV to modern movies. The inspiration for the show came from SCTV, an ensemble-based sketch series that featured Canadian comics such as John Candy (1950–1994), Eugene Levy (1946–), and Martin Short (1950–). As Stiller remembered in a BBC interview, he used to spend hours watching SCTV as a kid: "It was one of the shows that my parents and I could watch together and enjoy."

Stiller's series may have been short-lived (it consisted of only thirteen episodes), but it definitely served as the launching pad for the young entertainer's career. It also helped launch the careers of several other hip, young comics, including Andy Dick (1965–) and Janeane Garofalo (1964–), who would collaborate with Stiller on many future projects. In addition, Stiller's directing skills were honed. As his then-

Stiller and Wilson: On-Screen Duo

Ben Stiller and Owen Wilson have appeared in six movies together. They are:

The Cable Guy, 1996.

Permanent Midnight, 1998.

Meet the Parents, 2000.

Zoolander, 2001.

The Royal Tenenbaums, 2001.

Starsky & Hutch, 2004.

girlfriend Jeanne Tripplehorn told Jess Cagle of *Entertainment Week-ly,* "I always thought the Fox show was Ben's film school. When he would do those [film parodies], he would research the exact style of the directors and learn how they worked." The show was cancelled in 1992, but Stiller felt somewhat vindicated a year later, when he nabbed an Emmy Award (the highest achievement in television) for best writing in a variety or music series.

His Emmy win cleared the way for Stiller's big-screen project of 1994, *Reality Bites,* a film about a group of twenty-somethings in Houston, Texas, who face the trials and tribulations of life after college. Stiller directed the movie and co-starred in it along with Ethan Hawke (c. 1970–), Winona Ryder (1971–), and pal Garofalo. The film received mixed reviews and did poorly at the box office, but it was embraced by younger fans who saw it as a very real look at the post baby-boom generation, known as Generation X. It became a video cult classic and Stiller earned a reputation as a promising young independent film director. An independent film (also known as an indie film) is one that is low budget and usually made outside the big Hollywood studio system.

Stiller gives Wilson his first movie role

Over the next several years Stiller proved that he could work equally well on independent or big-budget projects, although he received the most acclaim for his indie affiliations. For example, the studio-backed *If Lucy Fell* (1996), which he co-starred in with Sarah Jessica Parker (1965–), was considered to be forgettable, but critics felt that Stiller gave a shining performance in the much smaller *Flirting with Disaster,* also from 1996. That same year, the actor returned to the director's chair and put a dark spin on a movie that what was supposed to be a goofy comedy, *The Cable Guy.* Originally written as another wacky vehicle for comic Jim Carrey (1962–), Stiller originally passed on the project. But, after Judd Apatow (c. 1968–), a former writer for *The Ben Stiller Show,* came on board, he and Stiller retooled the script and turned it into a darker, edgier film. Fans, however, were not expecting such a dark performance by Carrey and *Cable Guy* sagged at the box office. *The Cable Guy* also featured Owen Wilson in his first film role.

Owen Cunningham Wilson was born on November 18, 1968, in Dallas, Texas, the middle son of Robert, an ad executive, and Laura, a photographer. Older brother Andrew and younger brother Luke would also one day go into show business. The Wilsons, however, were not sure what would become of young Owen, who was a self-described trouble-maker. He earned horrible grades in school, had his famous nose broken in the ninth trade, and was expelled from school for cheating. As a result, Wilson was shipped off to a military academy in New Mexico. "At that point," he admitted to Amy Longsdorf of the *Morning Call,* "my mom and dad never thought I'd amount to anything." After high school, Wilson attended the University of Texas at Austin where he majored in English. He also met his future writing partner, Wes Anderson (1969–).

In 1992 Wilson and Anderson wrote, directed, and produced a short film called *Bottle Rocket,* about three friends who set out on a crazy crime spree. The movie was accepted at the Sundance Film Festival (an annual festival in Utah that supports emerging and independent films), and eventually made its way to the desk of veteran producer and writer James L. Brooks (1940–). Brooks agreed to back a full-length version of *Bottle Rocket,* which was released in theaters in 1996. The movie made only $1 million at the box office, but it was widely praised by critics. Based on *Bottle Rocket*'s poor showing, Wilson almost decided to throw in the towel. Friends in the industry, including Ben Stiller, convinced him otherwise. In 1996, Stiller offered Wilson a role in *The Cable Guy.* That same year, Wilson and Anderson collaborated as writers for the second time, which resulted in the critical and box-office success *Rushmore.*

In 1997 Stiller signed a multimillion-dollar deal with Fox to direct at least two feature films for their Fox 2000 division, and in the late 1990s Stiller seemed to have his pick of movie roles. The parts he chose were wildly different, and showed that the actor definitely had a range of styles. In 1998, for example, he co-starred in *Permanent Midnight,* a disturbing film based on the life of TV writer Jerry Stahl (c. 1954–), who also happened to be a heroin addict. The movie received so-so reviews, but Stiller was singled out for his role. As *People Weekly* enthused, Stiller turned in an "intense, take-no-prisoners performance." *Midnight* made friends out of Stiller and Stahl, who would work together again in the 2000s; the movie also featured Wilson in a small role.

The year 1998 also saw Stiller in *There's Something About Mary,* an over-the-top comedy written, produced, and directed by the Farrelly

Owen Wilson (left) and Ben Stiller in a still from the movie Zoolander *(2001).* Paramount/NVP/Red Hour/Village R'Show/The Kobal Collection/Gordon, Melinda Sue.

Brothers, known for such creations as *Dumb and Dumber* (1994). Most critics felt it was nothing more than a gross-out comedy that depended on crude jokes and physical humor, but moviegoers disagreed and turned it into the sleeper hit of the year. It was also the first project that Stiller was attached to that brought in big bucks at the box office; *Mary* took in $130 million during its first two months in theaters.

A "royal" partnership

Following the success of *Rushmore,* Wilson remained firmly planted in Hollywood. Known for his unconventional good looks and his unique, low-key acting style, he was cast in movie after movie, including *The Haunting* (1999), *Shanghai Noon* (2000), and *Behind Enemy Lines* (2001). By the time Wilson co-starred with Stiller in 2004's *Starsky & Hutch,* he was bringing in $10 million per picture. The former troublemaker from Texas also continued to add to his writing credentials. In 2001, he and Anderson penned their third film, *The Royal Tenenbaums.*

Into the 2000s, Stiller appeared in a string of comedies, the first of which was the hit *Meet the Parents* (2000), in which Wilson also had a role. He then joined Wilson for *The Royal Tenenbaums* (2001), playing Chas Tenebaum, the financial wizard in a family of child prodigies. Wilson's brother, Luke, appeared as Richie Tenenbaum, a tennis champion, and Gwenyth Paltrow rounds out the Tenenbaum siblings as the adopted sister Margot, a gifted playwright. Veteran actor Gene Hackman plays their father, Royal, who, after having deserted his family years ago, returns to make peace with his ex-wife and children. The film earned Wilson an Academy Award nomination for best original screenplay.

Stiller in turn tapped Wilson for *Zoolander* (2001), which Stiller also directed and co-wrote. The story, which Lisa Schwarzbaum of *Variety* called "90 minutes of elaborate comedic silliness," is a parody of the modeling world that centers on male model Derek Zoolander, a character originally created by Stiller in 1996. Although Schwarzbaum acknowledged that Stiller was a master at "skewering showbiz fabulousness," she, like most critics, also panned *Zoolander* for being a "feature-film dud."

Although *Zoolander* did not fare well in theaters, it did prove that Stiller was a master at creating a stellar ensemble cast of friends and family members, a trend that would continue throughout the 2000s. In addition to Wilson, who co-starred as Hansel, Stiller's rival, the movie featured Stiller's parents, sister Amy, wife Christine Taylor (whom he married in 2000), and a slew of acting buddies, including Andy Dick, Vince Vaughn (1970–), and Will Ferrell (1968–). Based on Stiller's star power, the DreamWorks film studio inked a three-year deal with the hot young comedian who now operated his own production company called Red Hour Films. As a result, in 2004 Stiller's plate was more than full. He starred in four movies, *Along Came Polly, Envy,* and *Dodgeball: A True Underdog Story.* His fourth film of 2004 was *Starsky & Hutch,* which co-starred Wilson.

By the end of 2004, Stiller had completed *Meet the Fockers,* the sequel to the 2000 hit *Meet the Parents.* He was also hard at work on a project that had been a dream of his for several years, a screen adaptation of the novel *What Makes Sammy Run,* written by Bud Schulberg. In 2004 Wilson wrapped up production on *The Wendell Baker Story,* a family affair since Wilson wrote the script with brother Luke. The movie was also co-directed by Luke and older brother Andrew. He also teamed with director Wes Anderson once again for *The Life Acquatic* (2004).

For More Information

Periodicals

Cagle, Jess. "Master of 'Disaster' Ben Stiller." *Entertainment Weekly* (April 19, 1996): pp. 50–54.

Dargis, Manohla. "Interview with Ben Stiller." *Interview* (April 1996): pp. 40–43.

Longsfort, Amy. "Interview with Owen Wilson." *Morning Call* (Allentown, PA) (February 14, 1999): p. F1.

"Review of *Permanent Midnight.*" *People Weekly* (September 28, 1998): p. 39.

Schwarzbaum, Lisa. "Pret-a-Passe: Ben Stiller's Clueless Male Model Tries to Play Hero in Zoolander, a High-Fashion Comedy That's So Last Year." *Entertainment Weekly* (October 5, 2001): p. 107.

Stein, Joel. "He's With Him: Ben Stiller and Owen Wilson Have Made Six Films Together. In Hollywood, Some Marriages Don't Make It That Far." *Time* (March 8, 2004): p. 70.

Wolk, Josh. "Stiller Standing." *Entertainment Weekly* (December 5, 2003): p. 75.

Web Sites

Adler, Shaun. "Interview: Owen Wilson and Ben Stiller of Starsky and Hutch." *Cinema Confidential News* (March 1, 2004) http://www.cinecon.com/news.php?id=0403011 (accessed on August 20, 2004).

Papamichael, Stella. "Ben Stiller: Starsky and Hutch." *BBC Online: Films* (March 12, 2004) http://www.bbc.co.uk/films/2004/03/12/ben_stiller_starsky_and_hutch_interview.shtml (accessed on August 20, 2004).

Stiller, Ben. "Interview with Ben Stiller." By Todd Gilchrist. *Blackfilm.com* (June 2004) http://www.blackfilm.com/20040618/features/benstiller.shtml (accessed on August 20, 2004).

Patricia Head Summitt

June 14, 1952 • Henrietta, Tennessee

Women's basketball coach

Pat Summitt, head coach of Tennessee University's women's basketball team, the Lady Vols, is one of the most successful coaches in collegiate basketball history. She has won six NCAA titles—only John Wooden, former coach of the men's basketball team at UCLA has won more, with ten NCAA championships to his credit. Summitt began her career as a college basketball player, later playing in two Olympics. Hard work, drive, and determination have led her to over eight hundred career wins in less than thirty years.

Learns work ethic on the farm

Summit was born Patricia Head on June 14, 1952, in Henrietta, Tennessee. She was the fourth child and only daughter of Richard and Hazel, who ran a farm. Summitt participated in all the chores necessary on a farm, and learned how to hold her own against her older brothers. She also learned basketball from them. Most evenings, after completing their chores, she and her brothers would climb the twenty-foot barn ladder to the top of the hayloft and play two-on-two basketball. She loved the game but, once she reached high school, she found out that her school district did not offer girls' basketball. Her father, supportive of her talent, moved the family across the county line to a school district that had girls' basketball.

Summit graduated from Cheatham County High in Ashland, in 1970. She then attended the University of Tennessee-Martin, earning a bachelor's degree in physical education in 1974. As a college student, she played with the Lady Pacers, the university's women's basketball team. As a junior she played in the U.S. World University Games, held

....

"I tell kids … 'If you're lazy, stay as far away from me and our program as you can because you'll be miserable.' We work hard."

in the Soviet Union, winning the silver medal. She hoped to play on the U.S. Olympic team, but those hopes were nearly dashed when, during her senior year, she suffered a knee injury. An orthopedic surgeon told Summitt that she would not be able to play basketball again. But Summitt would not give up. Strengthened by her father's insistence that the doctor "needed to fix her knee because she was going to the Olympics," Summit told her best friend, according to *Sports Illustrated,* "That doctor's crazy as heck if he thinks I'm not going to play ball again!" The upcoming 1976 Olympics in Montreal, Canada, would be the first time that women would play Olympic basketball, and Summitt did not want to miss out in this historic opportunity.

After graduation, she was offered a job as the women's basketball assistant coach for her alma mater. After the head coach quit to pursue Ph.D. studies, Summit, just twenty-two years old, was made head coach. She had never coached a game before and had no assistant coach. But she pushed her fear aside and threw herself into this new challenge. In addition to coaching, she also worked on her master's degree and taught physical education courses. At the same time, she worked on healing her knee and training herself for her Olympic dream. She worked out twice a day, losing twenty-seven pounds. Within a year, her knee was well enough for her to compete in the 1975 Pan American Games. The U.S. team won the gold medal. She was then named to the U.S. Olympic team and selected co-captain. The team claimed the silver medal in Montreal.

Wins first NCAA Championship

Summitt returned to her duties as head coach of the University of Tennessee-Martin's Lady Volunteers (often called simply the Lady Vols), guiding the team to the National Collegiate Athletic Association (NCAA) Final Four. The Lady Vols finished 16-8 that season. Summitt continued to play herself throughout the rest of the 1970s, playing in the World Championships and the Pan American Games. She looked forward to the 1980 Olympics in Moscow, but was forced to sit this Olympics out, since the United States boycotted the 1980 games in protest of the 1979 Soviet invasion of Afghanistan. But in 1984 Summitt went to the Olympics once again, this time as a coach. The U.S. team won the gold medal, securing its place in history as the first U.S. women's basketball team to take home the gold.

Her coaching success continued at the University of Tennessee, where she won the NCAA championships in 1987 and 1989. She was then granted the Basketball Hall of Fame's highest honor, the John Bunn Award. This 1990 award marked the first time that a woman had been so honored. In the 1990s the Lady Vols won four NCAA championships: 1991, 1996, 1997, and 1998. The team became the first women's basketball team ever to win three NCAA titles in a row.

With six NCAA championships under her belt, Summitt was recognized with numerous awards. She was named coach of the year three times by the Southeastern Conference (SEC)—1993, 1995, and 1998. She became the first women's college basketball coach to grace the cover of *Sports Illustrated* in 1997. The following year she was named both the Naismith Coach of the Year and the *Sporting News* Coach of the Year. In 1999 she was inducted into the Women's Basketball Hall of Fame. Summitt was subsequently inducted into the Basketball Hall of Fame in 2000, only the fourth women's basketball

Pat Summitt (center), with the Tennessee Lady Vols after her 800th career win, January 14, 2003. AP/ Wide World Photos. Reproduced by permission.

coach to be inducted. Also in 2000 she was named the Naismith Coach of the Century. Despite all these awards, Summitt would not accept full credit for the success of the Lady Vols. "It bothers me that there is so much focus on me...." she told Antonya English of the *St. Petersburg Times*. "It's about players; put the focus on the players."

Expects much from her players

The success of her players, however, is due in part to the high expectations Summitt has for them. She demands that they perform well academically, and insists they sit in the first three rows of their classes. Every player who has stayed with the Tennessee program has graduated. Her players describe Summitt as a harsh taskmaster, but also very caring. She pushes them to excel, and instills in them the same strong work ethic that she first learned on the family farm. According to her profile on the University of Tennessee Women's Collegiate Athletics Web Site, she "constantly challenges them to reach their potential as a student and an athlete."

In January of 2003 Summitt became the first female coach to win eight hundred games. The following season she coached her one-thousandth game. Summitt is also the coauthor of two books; *Reach for the Summitt* (1998) is a motivational book, and *Raise the Roof* (1998) chronicles the Lady Vols' undefeated 1998 season. More than that, the book, said Summitt according to *Sports Illustrated,* "is about trading in old, narrow definitions of femininity for a more complete one. It's about exploring all the possibilities in yourself." Ron Fimrite noted in *Sports Illustrated* that the book "represents a gratifying breakthrough in the literature of women's sports."

Additionally, Summitt is involved in numerous community organizations. She is a spokesperson for the United Way, Juvenile Diabetes, and Race for the Cure. She also serves as spokesperson for Verizon Wireless' HopeLine Program, which collects used cell phones, resells or recycles them, and donates the proceeds to victims of domestic violence. In 1980 she married R. B. Summitt, a bank executive. The couple lives in Knoxville, Tennessee, with one son, Ross Tyler Summitt.

For More Information

Periodicals

English, Antonya. *St. Petersburg Times* (March 9, 1999): p. 1C.

Fimrite, Ron. "Sky's the Limit." *Sports Illustrated* (November 16, 1998): p. 15.

Smith, Gary. "Eye of the Storm." *Sports Illustrated* (March 2, 1998).

Web Sites

"Pat Summitt Profile." *University of Tennessee Women's Collegiate Athletics.* http://utladyvols.collegesports.com/sports/w-baskbl/mtt/summitt_pat00.html (accessed on August 25, 2004).

"Patricia Head Summitt." *Biography Resource Center Online*. Gale Group, 1999. http://galenet.galegroup.com/servlet/BioRC (accessed on August 25, 2004).

Amber Tamblyn

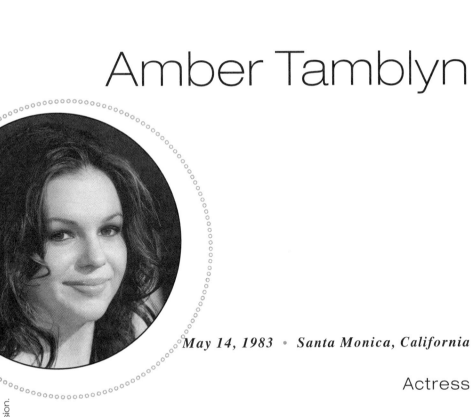

May 14, 1983 • Santa Monica, California

Actress

Most people talk to God in the privacy of their own homes, but when Amber Tamblyn talks to God she does it while eleven million other people watch. As the star of the surprise CBS television hit *Joan of Arcadia,* the twenty-one-year-old Tamblyn plays Joan Girardi a normal teenager who just happens to have the extraordinary ability to have one-on-one conversations with the "man upstairs." Considering the onslaught of reality-based programming, *Joan* was considered to be a refreshingly intelligent drama, and its star was viewed as one of the most promising newcomers on TV. Tamblyn, however, was actually a television veteran who virtually grew up on the small screen where, from age eleven to age seventeen, she played Emily Quartermaine on the long-running daytime soap opera, *General Hospital.* In the mid-2000s, Tamblyn was also broadening her fan base because of her activism. A vocal advocate for such diverse causes as autism and voting, she redefined the definition of what it means to be a modern celebrity.

Showbiz family

Amber Tamblyn's show biz connections go way back. Her paternal grandfather, Eddie Tamblyn, was a vaudeville headliner and a film star of the 1930s; her father, Russ Tamblyn, (1935–) is a legendary song-and-dance man known for his roles in such movie musicals as *Seven Brides for Seven Brothers* (1954) and *West Side Story* (1961). Prior to becoming a teen counselor, mother Bonnie pursued a career as an artist and sang lead in a rock band called Blue Heaven and the Rainbow Girl. As Tamblyn commented to *Soap Opera Weekly,* "All you have to do is smush them together and you have me."

> **"I think young girls should have someone to look up to who has a brain and ideas."**

When Amber Rose Tamblyn was born on May 14, 1983, in Santa Monica, California, she not only inherited her parents' show business genes, she also inherited an extended family in the form of her parents' celebrity friends. Tamblyn grew up around such Hollywood heavyweights as actor Dennis Hopper (1936–) and music great Neil Young (1945–), and listening to their stories, and those of her famous father, fueled an early interest in performing. From the age of five she attended an experimental school in California called the Santa Monica Alternative Schoolhouse, also known as SMASH. It was a creative arts center, with a focus on theater. While a student at SMASH, Tamblyn appeared in over thirteen plays, including a starring turn as Pippi Longstocking when she was in the fourth grade. Longstocking is the pigtailed character featured in books by children's author Astrid Lindgren (1907–2002). It was this particular play that helped launch Tamblyn's own celebrity.

Longtime family friend and casting agent Sharon Debord caught a performance of the play, and was so impressed that she urged the Tamblyns to let Amber go out on a few auditions. At first Russ Tamblyn was reluctant. He knew about the pitfalls of the business and did not want his daughter to be hurt or disappointed. "I wanted her to

Joan of Arc: Patron Saint of France

Joan of Arcadia is a very modern twist on the story of Joan of Arc, a peasant girl-turned-soldier who lived in France during the 1400s. Joan of Arc, or Jeanne d'Arc in French, was born circa 1412, the third child of Jacques D'arc, a farmer, and his wife, Isabelle de Vouthon. Joan had a very ordinary childhood. She spent her days tending her father's sheep, studying religion, and learning housekeeping skills from her mother. But, when she was twelve years old, she began to hear voices, which she believed came from messengers of God. According to Joan, these messengers told her that it was her mission to help free her country from English rule. At the time England dominated a portion of the country and the infant English king Henry VI (1421–1471) was proclaimed ruler of France.

The voices ordered Joan to cut her hair, dress in a soldier's uniform, and take to the battlefield. The people of France were convinced that her mission was divinely inspired and Joan was named a captain in the French army. In 1429 she led her troops to victory in the battle of Orleans, where the English were defeated and ultimately Charles VII (1403–1461) assumed his rightful role as the French monarch. At his coronation, Joan was given a place of honor. In 1430, however, she was captured and sold to the English. The next year, 1431, the young heroine was accused of being a witch and a heretic (someone who challenges the beliefs of the Church). After fourteen months of being questioned and tortured she was found guilty by the English court. On May 30, 1431, at the age of nineteen, Joan of Arc was burned at the stake. She was eventually found to be innocent of all charges, and she was made a saint of the Roman Catholic Church in 1920. Today she is considered to be a patron saint of France and is known as the Maid of Orleans.

grow up first," he explained to Anne Marie Cruz of *People*. "I thought auditions would burn her out." But, after some persistent nagging from Debord, Russ relented, and within just a few months Tamblyn had landed small roles in three indie films: *Biker Poet* (1994), *Rebellious* (1995), and *Live Nude Girls* (1995).

A soap opera favorite

In the winter of 1994, when she was just eleven years old, Tamblyn auditioned for the daytime soap opera *General Hospital (GH)*. The role of Emily Quartermaine was originally supposed to be short-term, but Tamblyn quickly became a favorite of fans and she ended up spending the next seven seasons playing the sweet, but often rebellious Emily. Going from California schoolgirl to full-time actress was not easy at first. "I couldn't play or go to birthday parties anymore," Tamblyn revealed to Cruz. "It was hard not to have relations with kids my age." As she grew older trying to maintain a balance between working and being a regular teenager became even harder. Life on the soap meant getting up at dawn, going to work at 6 A.M., and not returning home until about 8 o'clock at night. Given such a grueling schedule, Tamblyn's regular life was not so regular. While she attended public school some of the time, Tamblyn also had a teacher on the set. And, instead of going to pep rallies and proms like most kids, Tamblyn was busy promoting the soap at special events around the country and giving interviews to the press.

At the same time Tamblyn was growing by leaps and bounds as an actress. Emily was regularly featured in prominent storylines, many of which involved hard-hitting topics. First her mother died of cancer, and later a teenage Emily battled a drug addiction. Fans of all ages responded positively to the character's ups and downs, and eventually Tamblyn became one of the most popular actresses on *GH*. In addition, critics regularly praised Tamblyn for her insightful and mature performance. As Linda Susman of *Soap Opera Weekly* commented, "Since her early days on the soap, Tamblyn has consistently demonstrated a grasp of material that might be tricky for someone so young. She has elevated herself from child actor to peer in a cast of exceptionally talented players." Tamblyn also received several honors for her portrayal of Emily, including two awards given by the *Hollywood Reporter* for Best Young Actress in a Daytime Series.

In 2001, just before she turned eighteen, Tamblyn faced a triple whammy: she graduated from high school, she moved out of her parents' house to live on her own, and she decided to leave the comfort of her TV family on *General Hospital*. The decision was not an easy one since had been with the show since she was eleven years old. But, after going back and forth with her agent and her mother, Tamblyn made up her mind that it was time to go. "There comes a point in every actor's life," she explained to Rosemary Rossi of *Soaps in Depth,* "where they reach a stepping stone, and they have a choice to go around it or step up on it to see what the higher land can bring them." She also added, however, that the step was a bit frightening. "I'm coming out of the nest" she told Rossi. "Big time."

The divine Miss Joan

Toward the end of her *General Hospital* stint, Tamblyn had auditioned for roles on film and television, but her hectic schedule forced her to pass on more than one choice offer. Once free of her contract, she quickly landed guest spots on several prime time television shows, including *Buffy the Vampire Slayer, Boston Public,* and *CSI: Miami.* Tamblyn also snagged a small role in the big-screen thriller *The Ring* (2002). In spring of 2002, however, the actress hit the jackpot when she joined the cast of a new television drama called *Joan of Arcadia.* "I was going to do another project," Tamblyn told James Brady of *Parade,* "but I was blown away by the script. I fell in love with Joan at first sight."

The show premiered in September of 2003, and became an immediate, and unexpected, hit for CBS. Critics were surprised because of the slightly bizarre premise: an average teenager named Joan Girardi becomes not so average when she develops the ability to talk directly to God, who appears each week in the guise of a different person. God could be the lunch lady, a TV newscaster, and once God was even played by Tamblyn's real-life father, Russ. Also in the cast were veteran actors Mary Steenburgen (1953–) and Joe Mantegna (1947–), who portrayed Joan's parents, Helen and Joe Girardi, newcomer Michael Welch as younger brother Luke, and Jason Ritter, who played older brother Kevin. Ritter is the son of late comedic actor John Ritter (1948–2003).

Producing a show about religion could have been dicey. As Tamblyn remarked to Lynette Rice of *Entertainment Weekly,* "As soon as the word God comes out of your mouth, people are like, 'Uh-oh.'" But creator Barbara Hall, who was also responsible for launching the CBS program *Judging Amy,* had a very specific vision in mind: nothing preachy and something that would connect with young viewers. Joan is a typical modern teenager who doubts a great deal of things, but when she is directed by "God" to perform such simple acts as building a boat in her family's garage, the outcome is usually unexpected. Finding just the right person to portray the skeptical but open-minded Joan might also have been a challenge. "This girl's got to come off like a high schooler with the mind of a 50-year-old," Joe Mantegna explained to Rice.

Apparently Tamblyn fit the bill perfectly. By 2004 eleven million viewers were tuning in each week to catch Joan chatting with God, and critics were heaping praise on the show and its young star. The program captured both the People's Choice Award for Favorite New Dramatic Series and was named a top 10 TV Program of the Year by the American Film Institute. In December of 2003, Tamblyn was

nominated for a Golden Globe for Best Performance by an Actress in a Television series and in July of 2004, she snagged an Emmy nomination as Best Actress in a Series (Drama). At twenty-one, Tamblyn became the second-youngest actress to be nominated in this category. Claire Danes (1976–) was nominated for the award in 1995 for her work on *My So-Called Life*; she was sixteen at the time.

The cast of **Joan of Arcadia** *pose backstage with their Favorite New TV Dramatic Series People's Choice Award. Pictured left to right: Jason Ritter, Amber Tamblyn, Joe Mantegna, Mary Steenburgen, and Michael Welch.* AP/ Wide World Photos. Reproduced by permission.

Amber the activist

Although she achieved fame and fortune at a young age, Tamblyn is not the usual Hollywood celebrity. In interviews she is described as mature and wise beyond her years, and, instead of discussing fashion or film and television roles, she tends to steer the conversation to other topics. One such topic is politics, which Tamblyn is particularly passionate about. In 2004, she was able to vote for the first time in a presidential election and she took it very seriously. "We are so lucky to live in a country where we can have a say," Tamblyn commented to Alex Simon of *Venice*. "I call it the Power of One." The young activist was so inspired that she worked closely with MTV and its Rock the Vote campaign, which is targeted at getting young people interested in voting. Tamblyn also made a special appearance at the Rock the Vote party held in Boston, Massachusetts, on the eve of the Democratic National Convention.

In addition to her political involvement, in 2004 Tamblyn became a spokesperson for the Achievable Foundation, a Los Angeles-based group that offers support to people who are developmentally disabled, as well as to their families. This includes individuals who suffer from autism (a brain disorder that causes an inability to communicate or socially interact) or cerebral palsy (a brain disorder that affects communication between the brain and the muscles).

When not acting or working for a favorite cause, Tamblyn takes time to pursue her wide-range of hobbies, including writing and singing. She has already self-published two small books of poetry, *Of the Dawn* and *Plenty of Ships,* and has a longer volume in the works. Tamblyn also recorded a single called "God and Me," which was inspired by her television series. In the immediate future, the young star plans to continue her acting career. Her first starring role will be in *Sisterhood of the Traveling Pants,* based on the popular novel of the same name, and slated for a 2005 release. What's next for the multi-talented Tamblyn is anyone's guess. Perhaps college. As she laughingly remarked to Alex Simon, "Maybe when I'm about 30, after I've conquered the world, ended the war, and stopped world hunger, maybe I'll be able to take a few classes then!"

For More Information

Periodicals

Cruz, Anne Marie. "Hollywood and Divine: Amber Tamblyn, a Free Spirit in Real Life, Communes with God on the New Drama Joan of Arcadia." *People Weekly* (October 27, 2003): p. 93.

"Performer of the Week: Amber Tamblyn." *Soap Opera Digest* (February 2001): p. 12.

Rossi, Rosemary. "Growing Up and Moving Out." *Soaps in Depth* (July 24, 2001): pp. 98–101.

Rice, Lynette. "Holy Roller: *Joan of Arcadia* is a Heaven-Sent Gift for CBS and Its Fetching Young Star—and an Act of God for Its Creator." *Entertainment Weekly* (November 7, 2003): p. 36.

Simon, Alex. "Artist, Actor, Activist: Amber of Arcadia Raises the Bar." *Venice* (March 2004): pp. 63–65.

Susman, Linda. "Applause, Applause: Amber Tamblyn." *Soap Opera Weekly* (July 1, 1997): p. 29.

Web Sites

Amber Tamblyn Official Homepage. http://www.amtam.com/ (accessed on August 14, 2004).

Brady, James. "In Step with Amber Tamblyn." *Parade Magazine: Parade Archive* (January 11, 2004) http://archive.parade.com/2004/0111/0111 _instepwith.html (accessed on August 14, 2004).

Lonnie Thompson

July 1, 1948 • *Gassaway, West Virginia*

Paleoclimatalogist

Scientist Lonnie Thompson is an authority on ice. For more than thirty years, he has crossed every type of terrain, weathered blistering heat and teeth-rattling cold, and climbed some of the world's highest mountains in order to collect and study ice. Thompson studies ice cores from mountaintops because they provide an historical map of the climate of a region; cores also give a glimpse into the future of our planet's health. In the mid-2000s, the paleoclimatologist (a scientist who studies past climates through geological history) made a startling discovery: ice caps on mountains such as Kilimanjaro in Tanzania were melting at an alarming rate, and could completely disappear in the very near future. As a result, in the late 2000s Thompson and his team raced to Africa, Asia, and South America in order to retrieve samples of endangered ice. As NASA director James Hansen explained to *Science* magazine, "If [Thompson] wasn't doing it, we'd lose those records forever. He's a sort of hero."

From coal country to ice caps

Lonnie G. Thompson was born on July 1, 1948, in Gassaway, a tiny city in a poor rural area of West Virginia. His parents never went to school beyond eighth grade, but young Lonnie had bigger aspirations. From a very early age he showed an interest in science and displayed the kind of curiosity that would serve him well as an adult. For example, Thompson set up a weather station in his family's barn and would make bets using his lunch money on whether or not it would rain. In the late 1960s, the budding scientist enrolled at Marshall University, located in Huntington, West Virgina, which meant he was the first member of the Thompson family to attend college. In 1970 he graduat-

> **"What we're doing is cashing in on a bank account that was built over thousands of years but isn't being replenished. Once it's gone, it will be difficult to reform."**

ed with a degree in geology with the intent of becoming a coal geologist. The decision was a practical one; Thompson told Kevin Krajick of *Science* magazine, "I hated poverty, and West Virginia's full of coal."

While at Marshall, Thompson also met his future wife, Ellen Mosley, who would one day become his research partner and who eventually became a renowned scientist in her own right. Following graduation, Thompson and Mosley headed to Ohio State University (OSU) in Columbus to pursue graduate degrees in geology. Thompson soon became involved in a research project at OSU's Institute of Polar Studies (later renamed the Byrd Polar Research Center) where scientists were analyzing ice cores brought back from polar regions, including Greenland and Antarctica. This was a field that was just in its infancy, and Thompson and Mosley were fascinated. By studying layers of ages-old ice, researchers were able to analyze the gases, chemical elements, and dust concentrations that had been captured over the course of thousands of years. The collected data revealed

The Day After Tomorrow: Fact or Fiction

In 2004 Hollywood tackled the problem of global warming in the action-packed thriller *The Day After Tomorrow,* starring Dennis Quaid as a paleoclimatologist who tries to save his son from weather gone out of control. Because of global warming there has been an abrupt climate change, which creates catastrophic natural disasters around the globe: grapefruit-size hail pelts Tokyo, Japan; blizzards hit New Delhi, India; and overnight, the temperature in New York City swings from hot to freezing, causing the ocean to swell up and swallow Manhattan. All of the weather shifts mark the beginning of the next Ice Age.

Film fans appreciated the movie's stunning special effects, but scientists took an interest in the film for another reason. Lonnie Thompson saw *The Day After Tomorrow* twice, and, as he said to Maren Dougherty of *National Geographic,* "It's definitely over the top. But at least it forces the American public to think about the climate." And the public *was* curious about how much truth there was hidden in the fiction. Stefan Lovgren of *National Geographic* spoke with Tom Prugh, a senior editor at the Worldwatch Institute, a Washington, D.C.-based research center that focuses on the environment. According to Prugh, "There is a kernel of truth" in the movie, "although it has been 'Hollywoodized'."

Prugh went on to explain that global warming does indeed exist and that over the last one hundred years the temperature of Earth has increased about 1° Fahrenheit. That may not sound like a great deal, but according to Prugh it is a significant amount of warming that could potentially have serious consequences. Temperature changes cause such things as a rise in ocean levels (water expands as it heats), an increase in the number and intensity of storms, and major flooding. Indirectly, climate changes may also result in the extinction of an entire species (of plants, insects, or animals.).

Prugh was quick to point out that, unlike the movie, such drastic climate changes do not occur overnight. But he also added that humans are "stepping on the accelerator" by adding to the gases that are trapped in the Earth's atmosphere. Burning coal, oil, and gasoline are some of the major culprits. So, even though *The Day After Tomorrow* is just a movie, climate change is a very real issue. And Prugh hopes that moviegoers will take something away from the theater: "I hope people understand that climate change is happening now. It's affecting everyone who is alive on the planet, and it will inevitably affect their children and their children's children." Prush also offered some simple everyday fixes. One suggestion is to turn off the light when you leave a room. Since more than half of the electricity generated in the United States comes from coal, turning off a light reduces the amount of carbon released in the air. Just think what would happen if a million people stopped to turn off the lights.

much about the history of a region, including what the air temperature was during a certain period, how wet or dry an area was, what kind of volcanic activity took place, even what kind of plants were prevalent based on the type of pollen that was floating around.

Because the field was so new and there were so few polar drilling expeditions, competition was fierce. Mosley managed to

carve a spot for herself in the OSU geology department and eventually became a senior investigator on Antarctic drilling projects. But
Thompson decided to forge into an even newer area of exploration,
which involved collecting ice samples from tropical regions of the
planet. At the time, no one believed that such areas could yield anything valuable; tropical ice simply was not old enough or stable
enough to hold long-term records. Thompson, however, was convinced that even in warmer climates, the elevation of ice caps was so
extreme that layers of snow and ice probably stay frozen long enough
to reveal all kinds of data. So, in 1974, he struck out for the Peruvian
Andes to take on his first project: the ice cap of Quelccaya.

Across five continents

With an elevation of over 18,000 feet, very few people (except local
sheepherders) had ever been near Quelccaya, and no one had ever
actually explored the massive ice mound. As he climbed higher and
higher, Thompson experienced firsthand the dangers of working at
such an extreme elevation; dangers that included horrendous
headaches, difficulty breathing, and searing heat from the sun. In
addition, the novice explorer faced another obstacle: the drills used in
polar exploration could not be used; they were too heavy and had to
be powered with a generator. Undaunted, Thompson worked with a
Nebraska engineer named Bruce Koci to design a lighter drill that
would run on solar energy. He also appealed to other researchers to
collaborate with him. In 1983 Thompson, Koci, and several other scientists made their way to the top of Quelccaya. The expedition also
included forty mules, donkeys, and horses.

By the end of ten weeks, Thompson's team had successfully
extracted two ice cores that contained enough dust and debris to docu-
ment regional weather back to 470 C.E. It was the first deep-core
drilling of a tropical glacier and the first real tropical ice record.
Researchers in other fields sat up and took notice of the discovery.
Archaeologists, in particular, were pleased because Thompson's
research helped scientifically validate theories about ancient cultures
(such as the Tiwanuka) who they believed had lived in the area. Geolo-
gists were interested, but not overly impressed; a fifteen-hundred-year-
old core was nothing compared to centuries-old polar ice. But Thomp-

lonnie thompson

son was far from finished. Over the next fifteen years he went on countless expeditions to prove his point that tropical ice exploration was valid. And, accompanying him on his trips were the core members of his Quelccaya crew, including Koci and climatologist Keith Mountain. As Mountain told Kevin Krajick, "We've all lost enough skin and blood that no one needs to be told what to do. Something breaks, we fix it. Trouble comes, we know to get out of the way."

Thompson and his team traveled to fifteen countries over five continents, climbing to some of the highest elevations ever to be explored. Along the way they encountered countless hurdles. In 1991 and 1992, while tackling the Guliya ice cap in western China, samples had to be carted across the Ghobi Desert in ancient trucks and kept cool with ice cream. A 1993 hike to Peru's highest peak, Huascarán, was so treacherous that the team ended up living at the drill site for fifty-three days, which resulted in perhaps the record for the longest time spent living at high elevation. And in 1997, before climbing to the Sajama ice cap in Bolivia, Thompson and crew had to participate in a ceremony with local tribesmen who believed it was necessary to appease the mountain deities. All of the efforts were worth it, however, as Thompson began to bring home ice cores that were full of information.

Amazing discoveries and bleak predictions

In late 1997 Thompson made what would prove to be his most important expedition to date when he led of team of researchers from the United States, China, Peru, Russia, and Nepal to explore the Dasuopo Glacier in Tibet. At 26,293 feet, it was, and remains, the world's highest ice-core project. Samples taken from the site yielded an amazingly comprehensive record of the region that spanned over one thousand years. Of particular note were the records that detailed the history of the South Asian Monsoon, which is a climate event that occurs in annual cycles across India, Pakistan, and west toward Africa. Changes in the monsoon cycle can lead to catastrophic droughts or flooding. Thompson's data indicated that a major shift occurred in 1790, which led to a significant drought that lasted for seven years. As a result, more than six hundred thousand people died in India alone.

In February of 2001, Thompson presented his amazing findings at an annual gathering of the American Association for the Advancement of Science. But he had just returned from an expedition to Mount Kilimanjaro in West Africa and he also had some alarming news to share: the ice cap on the mountain was disappearing at an incredible rate. According to Thompson's data, 82 percent of the ice cap had melted between 1912 and 2000, and the rate of disintegration was accelerating. He predicted that by 2015 the cap would be gone. Thompson also revealed that the same phenomenon was happening in other tropical areas as well. At Quelccaya, for example, the cap had shrunk by about one-fifth since he took his first trip there twenty-eight years before.

Some scientists claimed that the melting was due to a combination of natural and man-made factors. Thompson, however, directly linked the melting to accelerated global warming, which is the increased temperature of the earth caused by an increased density of gases (such as carbon monoxide) in the earth's atmosphere. "There is no question in my mind," Thompson explained in his report, which was featured in *Time* magazine, "that the warming is in part, if not totally, driven by human activity." He pointed to the fact that samples revealed a four-fold increase in dust trapped in the ice and a doubling of carbon monoxide concentrations. Thompson's most troubling revelation was that, based on the analysis of the ice from both Tibet and Africa, the last decade had been the warmest in one thousand years.

Thompson's personal mission

Although Thompson's findings come from the tropics, he feels that his predictions have a wide-reaching effect. "These tropical glaciers are an early-warning system for the climate of the Earth," he told Maren Dougherty of *National Geographic*. He went on to explain that addressing global warming is the responsibility of everyone: "It's just a matter of time before everyone will realize that we have to do something if we want to maintain the type of civilization we live in." As a result, Thompson and his wife have made it their personal mission to educate people from kids in grade school to university researchers that humans are warming the earth, but that it is not too late to do something about it.

Thompson also made it a personal mission to make marathon expeditions to endangered ice cap sites. "We've got to get these archives before they're gone," he commented to Ned Rozell of *Alaska*

Science Forum. In late 2004, Thompson returned to Quelccaya and the Himalayas, and he and his team scouted out at least thirteen other sites around the world, including peaks in Russia and one on Heard Island, a tiny spot in the Indian Ocean that has never been explored before. Although the science community finally acknowledged that tropical regions are crucial areas of research, funding for such projects was still hard to come by. As a result, Thompson began to seek some nontraditional methods of funding. For example, he has approached private donors such as media mogul Ted Turner (c. 1938–) and companies that focus on outdoor gear, including Lands' End.

In the meantime Thompson and his researchers at Ohio State University, where he is a full professor, study the ice samples that are housed in cold storage. The OSU storage facility is approximately 2,100 square feet and holds ice cores that, if laid end-to-end, would stretch over four miles. It is important to keep them, Thompson explained to *National Geographic,* because they are living archives. Such archives prove valuable to other researchers at other institutions, and they are important for the future. "Because it's clear," Thompson added, "that in as few as 15 years, you will not be able to go out into the real world to recover that record."

The Indiana Jones of scientists

Thompson's discoveries have made him a very famous man. He makes national headlines on a regular basis, he has been invited to the White House to share his expert opinions, and environmentalists consider him to be a spokesman for the planet. Fellow scientists sometimes doubt the exact timing of his predictions, but they also acknowledge Thompson as a geologist who is fiercely dedicated to his work. According to Harvard University geochemist Daniel Schrag, who spoke with Krajick, "He's the closest living thing to Indiana Jones." A strange description for the quiet, bespectacled Thompson, who does not consider himself to be an adventurer. "I only want the data," he admitted to Krajick. And Thompson seems determined to get the data regardless of his own personal safety. He has a minor heart-valve defect and in 1996 he was diagnosed with severe asthma. Both conditions could prove fatal for someone who climbs to elevated heights. But, as Ned Rozell put it, "Thompson will not rest while the ice is still there."

For More Information

Periodicals

Krajick, Kevin. "Ice Man: Lonnie Thompson Scales the Peaks for Science." *Science* (October 18, 2002): pp. 518–522.

Merrell, Lolly. "The Vanishing World of Lonnie Thompson." *National Geographic Adventure* (August 2004).

Reaves, Jessica. "The Dusty Rocks of Kilimanjaro Just Doesn't Have the Same Ring." *Time* (February 19, 2001).

Web Sites

Dougherty, Maren. "High-Climbing Ice Expert Gets to Core of Climate Change." *National Geographic Adventure* (July 27, 2004) http://news.nationalgeographic.com/news/2004/07/0727_040727_globalwarming.html#main (accessed on August 16, 2004).

Lovgren, Stefan. "Day After Tomorrow Ice Age Impossible, Researcher Says." *National Geographic News* (May 27, 2004) http://news.nationalgeographic.com/news/2004/05/0527_040527_DayAfter.html (accessed on August 17, 2004).

Rozell, Ned. "Where Science and High Adventure Meet." *Alaska Science Forum* (April 22, 2004) http://www.gi.alaska.edu/ScienceForum/ASF16/1695.html (accessed on August 17, 2004).

"Time Magazine, CNN Name OSU Geologist One of 'America's Best.'" Ohio State University Press Release. (August 13, 2001) http://www.osu.edu/osu/newsrel/Archive/01-08-13_Lonnie_Thompson_Time-CNN.html (accessed on August 17, 2004).

Wong, Kate. "Himalayan Ice Cores." *Scientific American Web site* (September 18, 2000) http://www.sciam.com/article.cfm?articleID=000D4E78-7113-1C61-B882809EC588ED9F (accessed on August 17, 2004).

Justin Timberlake

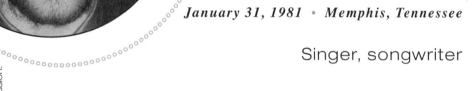

January 31, 1981 • *Memphis, Tennessee*

Singer, songwriter

In late 2002 Justin Timberlake managed to make the leap that many young stars never accomplish—the leap from teen idol to full-fledged, adult artist. In the late 1990s, he was one-fifth of the wildly popular boy band 'N Sync, considered to be the cute, funny one, and a headline maker thanks mostly to his on-again, off-again romance with pop princess Britney Spears. But, having hit the ripe old age of twenty-one, Timberlake decided to leave the safety of his supergroup to launch a solo career. His debut CD, called *Justified,* was released in December of 2002, and its funky mix of hip-hop and R&B clicked with both old fans and new. More importantly, Timberlake gained the respect of critics and peers. In 2003 he took home several awards for his freshman effort, including three MTV Video Music Awards, and in February of 2004, Timberlake snagged two Grammies, considered the highest achievement in the music industry. It seemed the pop idol had grown up, and as Jenny Eliscu commented in *Rolling Stone,* Timberlake "attained the one thing he wanted more than anything else: credibility."

From singing toddler to Mouseketeer

Justin Randall Timberlake was born on January 31, 1981, in Memphis, Tennessee, considered to be the home of the blues and the birthplace of rock and roll. From the very beginning, Timberlake's mother, Lynne, knew her son would be a performer. He was dancing along to the radio when he was just a toddler, and by the age of two and a half, Timberlake (nicknamed Curly) could sing in perfect harmony. As Timberlake later recalled in a *Time for Kids* interview, "Ever since I was a little boy I always sang. So I figured out that was sort of my calling."

When Timberlake was three his parents divorced. He remained friends with his father, but he grew up with his mother and his stepfa-

> **"**I know people have an image of me in their head, but I want them to be able to see past that. I want them to see the musicality of what I'm doing.**"**

ther, Paul Harless, who Lynne married when Timberlake was five years old. Young Justin was, and is, extremely close to his mother. In fact, he has a small tattoo on his back of an angel holding a banner that bears her initials. In addition, Lynne later became her son's manager. Timberlake started out singing in the church choir; he began his stage career by performing in countless local talent contests. In 1992, after several years of voice lessons, he appeared on *Star Search,* a televised tournament-style talent competition that helped launched the careers of many top entertainers. The eleven-year-old sang under the name of Justin Randall, and although he received high marks from the judges, he did not win the contest.

Timberlake was not discouraged. He continued to make the rounds of auditions, and in 1993, at age twelve, he landed a spot on *The Mickey Mouse Club,* a half-hour show for kids that blended singing, dancing, and comedy sketches. Competition to be a Mouseketeer was high, considering thousands of hopefuls tried out

The Justin Timberlake Foundation

Pop idol Justin Timberlake may spend his money freely on clothes, cars, and plenty of bling, but he is also committed to helping youngsters fulfill their dreams. In 2000 Timberlake established the Justin Timberlake Foundation, with the goal of funding and supporting music programs in public schools. As the performer told *Time for Kids,* "This is about an opportunity that every young person should enjoy, no matter what career they aspire to. I want to do everything I can to make sure other people can benefit from music education." In May of 2000, the foundation's first grant was awarded to Timberlake's own Memphis elementary school, E. E. Jeeter. In addition to money, the pop performer donates his time to help schools integrate music into the curriculum. He also helps others raise funds for what he considers to be an important initiative. For example, the foundation regularly auctions off items online, including Timberlake concert tickets and some of the star's own belongings, such as his sneakers.

In 2002, the Timberlake Foundation joined forces with the American Music Conference (AMC), a national, nonprofit organization, which according to its Web site at http://www.amc-music.org, is "dedicated to promoting the importance of music, music-making, and music education to the general public." That same year, Timberlake partnered with AMC to urge Congress to support music education in U.S. schools. Thanks to Timberlake's involvement, millions of people visited the AMC Web site, kids and adults wrote letters to their congressmen, and by late 2002, Timberlake's mother, Lynn Harless, delivered a petition containing thousands of signatures to Capitol Hill. As Timberlake explained on the AMC Web site: "The main purpose of this petition drive is to show the people on Capitol Hill how important music education is to the people they're working for. The publicity that surrounded the petition has reached millions of people and gotten them talking. I think we've laid a foundation for more public activism in the future, and I hope people start in their own home towns."

for the show, and Timberlake was thrilled to be added to the program. He and his mother moved to Orlando, Florida, where the series was produced, and for two years he appeared as a regular along with fellow cast members, including up-and-coming stars, Britney Spears (1981–), Christina Aguilera (1980–), and future bandmate Joshua Scott (J. C.) Chasez (1976–). When the show was cancelled in 1994, Timberlake was disappointed, but he already had his sights on his next move. He and Chavez had been contacted by a young singer named Christopher Kirkpatrick (1971–) who had seen them on *Mickey Mouse* and now wondered if the two ex-Mouseketeers would be interested in joining a band he was putting together. Timberlake and Chavez joined forces with Kirkpatrick, Joseph (Joey) Fatone (1977–), and Jason Allen Alexander (1981–) to become one of the most successful pop groups ever, 'N Sync.

Boy band history

The five young men formed instant friendships and it was clear that their harmonizing styles blended together perfectly. As a result, because they were so in sync, Timberlake's mother came up with the band's appropriate name. In addition, 'N Sync was formed from the last letter of each member's first name (Justin, Chris, Joey, Jason, and J. C.). When Lance Bass (1979–) replaced Jason Allen, the boys jokingly called him Lansten so he would fit into the group's acronym. In need of financial backing, the band turned to Lou Pearlman of the Trans Continental management company. Pearlman quickly put the boys in touch with Johnny and Donna Wright, who became 'N Sync's tour managers. The Wrights were music veterans with just the right experience; they had previously managed 1980's teen heartthrobs New Kids on the Block, and they had recently helped form the Backstreet Boys, another five-member teen vocal combo, and one that would be constantly compared to 'N Sync.

The rest is boy band history. 'N Sync began by touring extensively in Europe where they honed their vocals and on-stage choreography. In 1998 they released their self-titled debut album in the United States, as well as a Christmas album, *Home for Christmas,* and for the next three years they topped the pop charts, packed stadiums, and sold millions of records. Critics generally dismissed them as cookie-cutter bland, but millions of fans, most of them pre-teen girls, gobbled up everything 'N Sync. They plastered their walls with posters, bought 'N Sync dolls, bopped to dance numbers, such as "I Want You Back," and swooned over sugary-sweet ballads, including "God Must Have Spent a Little More Time On You." Thousands of Web sites and fan magazines popped up overnight and every girl had a favorite band member. Timberlake, in particular, was a fan favorite, perhaps because he was the youngest of the group. Or, maybe because of his much publicized relationship with Britney Spears, which made for constant tabloid fodder.

In 1999, after a bitter dispute, the band broke from Pearlman, who was accused of mismanaging funds. 'N Sync signed with Jive Records, and released two more albums: *No Strings Attached* (2000), which broke industry records when it sold 2.4 million copies in its first week of release, and *Celebrity* (2001), a blend of electronica, R&B (Rhythm and Blues), and country. The "boys" were definitely growing up, taking control, and proving that they had true staying power. They were also branching out on projects of their own. Bass and Fatone were acting in TV, film, and theater, Kirkpatrick launched a clothing line, and Chasez wrote and produced tracks for other recording artists. In 2001, however, when they officially took time out from the band to pursue individual ventures, Timberlake was the first to release a solo album.

Justin is justified

In interviews Timberlake reported that he wanted to do a solo record because he needed the freedom to express himself. He also claimed that the impetus was the breakup of his almost four-year relationship with Spears. "It was angst in the form of heartbreak," he told Jon Wiederhorn of MTV.com. "Writing a couple of songs on the record helped me deal with things. It was like a whole big spa treatment." Timberlake had the emotion, he had the singing chops, and he had some writing experience since he had penned several 'N Sync songs, including "Gone" and "Girlfriend." But he still needed collaborators, and although he was connected with Jive Records, producers still needed convincing to become connected with the boy with the bubble-gum past.

Timberlake was fortunate to snag some of the biggest names in the business, including Pharrell Williams and Chad Hugo of The Neptunes, producers of such hip-hop artists as Jay-Z, Mystikal, and Ludacris; Tim 'Timbaland' Mosely; Andre Harris; and Vidal Davis. Although these industry giants definitely laid the blueprint for the album, and their urban styles are evident in such tracks as "Nothin' Else" and "Last Night," *Justified* was undeniably Timberlake's own. He co-wrote each of the thirteen songs, and he injected his own sense of soul into each and every one. "As a kid, I gravitated toward Stevie Wonder, Al Green, and Marvin Gaye" the singer explained to Meredith Lerner of VH1.com, "and that stuff's still with me." By the end of the six weeks of recording, Timberlake's collaborators recognized that talent. As producer Scott Storch told Jon Wiederhorn, "[Timberlake] has a passion for classic soul music, and he's learned lots of tricks from back in the day that he's applying to modern music. He's sort of a return to blue-eyed soul."

Justified was released in November of 2002, and a nervous Timberlake wondered how it would be received. "I kind of feel like every-

Justin Timberlake performs in London, England. AP/Wide World Photos. Reproduced by permission.

body has their magnifying glasses out," he confessed to MTV.com. Critics, however, had nothing but praise for his solo effort. Polly Vernon of the *Guardian Unlimited* called it "inventive and instant…a truly great record," and described Timberlake's voice as "honey-dipped and sweet." Jon Wiederhorn praised, in particular, the track "Cry Me a River," stating that it "marked [Timberlake's] transformation from doe-eyed teenybopper to pained and relevant singer/songsmith." Reviewers also compared Timberlake to a young Michael Jackson (1958–) and many, including Jenny Eliscu of *Rolling Stone,* dubbed him the new king of pop.

All grown up

Timberlake had a whirlwind 2003, which he spent on the road performing and relentlessly promoting his album. In the summer he traveled throughout the United States and Europe with Christina Aguilera as part of the sold-out Justified and Stripped tour. He took a brief break to play a benefit concert in Toronto, Canada, sharing the stage with such legendary bands as the Rolling Stones, AC/DC, the Guess Who, and Rush. Timberlake was also a regular on the talk-show circuit and continued to make headlines, not as Britney Spears's boyfriend, but as the most popular performer of the moment. It seemed every move he made hit the news: he hosted *Saturday Night Live* in October of 2003, became part-owner of a Los Angeles-based restaurant in November of 2003, and of course his love life was not off limits. The twenty-two-year-old was romantically linked with actress Cameron Diaz (1972–), who is nine years his senior.

Timberlake also popped up on every music industry awards show imaginable, from the MTV Video Music Awards to the MTV Europe Music Awards to the American Music Awards, where he took home the prize for favorite pop album of the year. In February of 2004 the new solo artist even landed two surprise Grammy wins, including best pop vocal album and best male pop vocal performance for "Cry Me a River." In the latter category, he was up against such music mainstays as Sting (1951–), Michael McDonald (1952–), and George Harrison (1943–2001). Timberlake's Grammy glory was almost overshadowed by an event that took place earlier in the month: while performing with Janet Jackson (1966–) during halftime at Super Bowl XXXVIII, Timberlake stunned audiences when he yanked off the top of Jackson's outfit. Both artists later apologized and reported that it was a mistake caused by a costume malfunction.

By the end of 2004, there was no rest for Timberlake. When he did manage to take a few days off he went traveling with girlfriend Diaz, or headed to Memphis, where his parents still live in the brick Tudor-style house Timberlake grew up in. While there, he hangs out with his dogs Bearlie and Bella, plays pinball and Halo on his Xbox, and hits a few rounds of golf, which is his latest passion. Timberlake was also fielding offers from movie producers, who were keen on tapping into his talent. He signed on to make two movies, slated for released in 2005. The first, called *Edison,* features Timberlake as a young journalist who teams up with two veteran investigators played by Morgan Freeman (1937–) and Kevin Spacey (1959–). The second movie is *Wanna-Be,* which will star Timberlake as a college baseball prodigy. Rumors also abounded about whether or not the pop star-turned actor would be joining his 'N Sync bandmates on a new album. Timberlake remained noncommittal, telling the press that he was not sure if he was contractually obligated.

For More Information

Periodicals

Eliscu, Jenny. "The New King of Pop." *Rolling Stone* (December 25, 2003).

Hedegaard, Erik. "The Bachelor: Pop's Mr. Heartbreak Goes It Alone." *Rolling Stone* (January 23, 2003).

Web Sites

"Justin Timberlake: Wanna Be Starting Somethin'." *VH1.com: Artists* (June 16, 2003) http://www.vh1.com/artists/interview/1472671/06132003/timberlake_justin.jhtml (accessed on August 23, 2004).

Justin Timberlake Web site. http://www.justintimberlake.com/ (accessed on August 23, 2004).

Klueber, Jill. "Justin's Solo Act." *Time for Kids: Kid Scoops* (November 11, 2002) http://www.timeforkids.com/TFK/kidscoops/story/0,14989,389161,00.html (accessed on August 23, 2004).

Lerner, Meredith. "Justin Timberlake: Work in Progress." *VH1.com: Artists* (November 18, 2002) http://www.vh1.com/artists/interview/1458752/11182002/timberlake_justin.jhtml (accessed on August 23, 2004).

Vernon, Polly. "Boy Wonder." *Guardian Unlimited (UK)* (October 6, 2002) http://observer.guardian.co.uk/magazine/story/0,11913,804933,00.html (accessed on August 23, 2004).

Wiederhorn, Jon. "Why is Justin Timberlake the Only Youngster Who Can Stand Up to Sting?" *MTV.com: News* (February 2, 2004) http://www.mtv.com/news/articles/1484705/20040202/story.jhtml (accessed on August 23, 2004).

Gabrielle Union

October 29, 1973 • Omaha, Nebraska

Actress

While many who have seen her perform mention her beauty, natural ability, and star quality, Gabrielle Union did not set out to be an actress. After an internship in the office of a modeling agency during her college years, Union was invited to get in front of the camera. She gave it a try, and the modeling soon led to small roles in television shows. Those in turn led to small roles in feature films, and by 2000, just a few years after her first television appearances, Union had won a major role in the popular movie *Bring It On,* starring Kirsten Dunst (1982–). Since then she has been offered significant parts in a steady stream of films, including *Two Can Play That Game* (2001), *Deliver Us from Eva* (2003), and *Breakin' All the Rules* (2004). She costarred alongside Martin Lawrence (1965–) and Will Smith (1968–) in the 2003 blockbuster *Bad Boys II.* Not a bad resume for someone who had never studied acting and who once told Jeffrey Epstein of *E! Online* that she used to think acting was a "cheesy profession." Her list of accomplishments is even more impressive considering the general lack of decent roles for African American actors. In spite of poor odds, Union has forged a successful career, scoring one good role after another while at the same time maintaining a level head and a sharp sense of humor.

A Midwestern gal

Gabrielle Monique Union was born in Omaha, Nebraska, in 1973, the middle child in a family of three daughters. Her parents, Sylvester and Teresa, both worked as managers for the telecommunications company AT&T; her father also served in the military, reaching the rank of

> **"Hey, I'm just riding this train as long as I can. As long as I'm having fun, I'll do it. When it stops being fun, I'll try something else. Maybe I'll open up a chain of Popeye's Chicken."**

sergeant. Union's early childhood years were spent as part of a rich black community and as part of a large family that had been in the Omaha area for many generations. Her sense of belonging and connection to the community changed when Union was about eight years old. In 1981 her father was transferred, and the family moved to Pleasanton, a predominantly white suburban neighborhood in northern California. Union's mother made sure her daughters received an education in black culture and history, but Union still longed to have the companionship of other black girls. She told *Savoy* magazine, in an article that appeared on the *Gabrielle Union Fan Club* Web site, "I wanted the camaraderie. I can tell you anything you want to know about any [black] writer or about any event, but I didn't have the friendships." Her parents felt strongly that their daughters should hold onto family ties, and they often returned to Nebraska during her childhood summers. In spite of the fact that she has spent most of her life in California, Union still considers herself a Midwesterner.

During her high school years Union was a talented, hard-working athlete, excelling at soccer, track, and basketball. She also performed well in the classroom, making the dean's list at Foothill High in Pleasanton. Much of her motivation for success came from her father, who continually pushed her to improve. She recalled to Clarissa Cruz of *Entertainment Weekly* the type of lecture she often heard from her father: "You are the only black person in your whole class. You're gonna have to prove to them every day that you're just as smart, if not smarter. Just as good, if not better. Just as fast, if not faster." This placed twice the pressure on Union to succeed, as she told *Entertainment Weekly*, "So not only am I trying to beat all my classmates, I'm trying to prove to my dad that I'm living up to his expectations." After graduating, Union returned to her childhood hometown, attending the University of Nebraska in Lincoln (UNL). She went back to California after one semester, however, finding it hard to fit in socially at UNL. She attended one semester at Cuesta College in Southern California, but then dropped out, unsure what direction her life would take. In 1992, while trying to figure out what to do next, she took a summer job at a Payless shoe store, which would become the site of a horrifying incident.

One evening, as Union and another employee were closing the store, an armed man entered the store, emptied the cash register, and sexually assaulted Union at gunpoint. At one point she was able to get the gun, and attempted to shoot her attacker. The gun jammed, however, and the man beat her and then left the store. He later turned himself in, and Union eventually learned that he was an employee of another Payless store who had robbed several stores and previously raped another Payless employee. He was convicted of his crime against Union, and she went on to successfully sue Payless for their negligence and failure to warn employees of the man's prior crimes and his potential danger to other female workers. Traumatized by the attack, Union sought comfort from her oldest friends. She began meeting with a group of other sexual assault survivors, and for many years she gave talks in support of other victims.

Graduating to the silver screen

Union then moved on to complete her college education, graduating from the University of California in Los Angeles (UCLA) in 1996.

During her senior year at UCLA, Union sought to add additional credits to her regular class schedule by finding an internship. She became a
temporary office worker at a modeling agency, where clients repeated-
ly mistook her for one of the models. After she graduated, the agency
invited her to sign on with them as a model and Union agreed, eager to
begin paying off her student loans before entering law school. She
soon found herself gracing the pages of publications such as *Teen* magazine. After modeling for a short time, Union decided to try her hand at
acting. Her first audition, in 1996, resulted in a guest part on the television show *Saved by the Bell: The New Class.* Over the next few years,
Union won a succession of guest roles on such programs as *Moesha,
Sister, Sister,* and *ER.* She had a recurring role on *Seventh Heaven,* and
in 2001 made a landmark appearance on the long-running sitcom
Friends. Union, playing a woman who dates both Joey and Ross, had
the distinction of being the first minority love interest on the show.

In the midst of her steady television appearances, Union also
began winning small roles in feature films. She appeared in a string of
teen-oriented movies, including *She's All That, 10 Things I Hate
about You* (both released in 1999), and *Love and Basketball* (2000).
With her role as cheerleading captain Isis opposite Kirsten Dunst in
Bring It On (2000), Union crossed over into movie-star territory. She
trained hard for the role—gaining new respect for cheerleaders—and
brought to the character a sense of uncompromising inner strength.
The movie was a big hit, and Union found herself with millions of
new fans. Around the same time she scored a lead role on the short-
lived television series *City of Angels.* Union enjoyed her character, a
surgical resident in a Los Angeles hospital, but when the series was
canceled, her schedule could more easily accommodate film roles.
And the roles kept coming, with Union appearing in two major films
in 2001. Both films, *The Brothers* and *Two Can Play That Game,* featured black casts and dealt with issues of romance, commitment, and
faithfulness. In the midst of her busy schedule, Union managed to fit
in her wedding to Chris Howard, a former running back for the Jacksonville (Florida) Jaguars. Howard had moved to Los Angeles after
his football career ended, in order to be closer to Union. He became a
sports therapist and worked for the Fox Sports network.

Union encountered another busy year in 2002, appearing in two
films. In *Welcome to Collinwood,* which stars Luis Guzmán, William

H. Macy, Isaiah Washington, and Patricia Clarkson, Union portrays a young blind girl named Michelle. To research the role, she spent time with a blind woman at the Braille Institute. In *Abandon,* a campus thriller starring Katie Holmes and Benjamin Bratt, Union portrays a friend of Holmes's character. While both movies offered Union a chance to explore new types of roles, she longed for a more significant movie part.

The following year she got that role, playing the title character in *Deliver Us from Eva.* The film, loosely based on the play *The Taming of the Shrew* by English poet and playwright William Shakespeare (1564–1616), tells the story of eldest daughter Eva, who takes over as guardian of her three younger sisters after the death of their parents. She continues to exert control over their lives even as they reach adulthood, much to the dismay of their husbands and boyfriends. The men hatch a plot to stop Eva from meddling in their affairs. They pay a local ladies' man, portrayed by rapper/actor LL Cool J, to date Eva, make her fall in love with him, and then take her out of their lives. Naturally the plan is complicated when the playboy falls in love with Eva, and she with him. While reviewers offered only lukewarm praise for the film, it met with success at the box office, earning close to $20 million. The film's director, Gary Hardwick, offered warm praise for Union in an article in *Jet:* "She's a wonderful actress, very gifted and with marvelous comic timing. She's sexy, and she can make you laugh or she can make you cry. You want to watch her to see just exactly what she's going to do next. She has all the tools of a leading lady."

Also in 2003, Union appeared in *Cradle 2 the Grave,* an action movie starring martial arts star Jet Li, rapper DMX, and comedian Anthony Anderson. She also scored a significant role in *Bad Boys II,* one of the biggest hits of the summer of 2003, in which Union played the role of Syd, the half-sister of Martin Lawrence's character and the love interest for Will Smith's character. Union returned to the romantic comedy genre in 2004 with a starring role in *Breakin' All the Rules.* Also featuring Jamie Foxx and Morris Chestnut, *Rules* is a mistaken-identity romp that examines the absurd behavior of those desperate to maintain or get out of a relationship. Joe Leydon listed Union's charms in a *Daily Variety* review of *Rules,* writing that "Union once again evidences (as in *Deliver Us from Eva*) impressive range and star presence as she comes off smart and sexy, feisty and vulnerable."

Gabrielle Union (center) poses with Will Smith (left) and producer Jerry Bruckheimer at the Germany premiere of **Bad Boys II**. AP/Wide World Photo. Reproduced by permission.

Despite her increasingly high profile, Union has retained her down-to-earth personality. She appreciates the salaries she earns for her film roles and the recognition given for her work, but has tried to keep things in perspective. She shared advice for other young actors with Lori Talley of *Back Stage West:* "Don't just concentrate on the business.... Have a life outside of this and have other interests, because those are the things that keep you working."

Cruz praised Union's "Midwestern-girl-next-door sensibility that sets her apart from the fleet of glamourous starlets that regularly dock on Tinseltown shores." Union and her husband share a modest Los Angeles home with a mortgage that will still be manageable if the film roles suddenly dry up. She told Tom Gliatto of *People:* "If I had to go work as a social worker, I could still afford it. We squirrel away a lot. I don't live for today. I live for twenty years down the road." While Union prepares for plan "B"—saving money for her post-acting days—many fans and industry insiders look ahead with certainty to the day in the near future when Union will rise to the position of an A-list movie star.

For More Information

Periodicals

Cruz, Clarissa. "And They Call It Buppie Love." *Entertainment Weekly*
   (April 25, 2003): p. 70.

Gliatto, Tom. "Union's Dues." *People* (August 11, 2003): p. 75.

Leydon, Joe. *"Breakin' All the Rules." Daily Variety* (May 14, 2004): p. 2.

"LL Cool J & Gabrielle Union Star in Romantic Comedy *Deliver Us from Eva." Jet* (February 17, 2003): p. 58.

Talley, Lori. "Proud Model." *Back Stage West* (March 29, 2001): p. 7.

Web Sites

Epstein, Jeffrey. "Gabrielle Union: Bring It On." *E! Online.* http://www.eonline.com/Celebs/Who/gu.html (accessed on August 12, 2004).

"Gabrielle Union." *Savoy* (February 2000). Appears at *Gabrielle Union Fan Club.* http://www.gabrielleunionfanclub.com/articles/savoy.htm (accessed on August 12, 2004).

Peter Vitousek

January 24, 1949 • *Honolulu, Hawaii*

Ecologist

When he began his studies as a young man, Peter Vitousek had no plans to become one of the world's leading ecologists. The Hawaii native started out as a political science major, switching to ecology when he came across a book about the damage done to certain regions when new species of plants and animals are introduced and take over. After completing his education and becoming a university professor and research scientist, Vitousek eventually ended up in his home state, studying vegetation and wildlife in the hopes of preserving ecosystems—the interworkings of organisms and their surrounding environment—in Hawaii and around the world. One of the issues Vitousek has focused on involves the problem of too much nitrogen in the environment. Nitrogen is an element that occurs naturally, but it also enters soil and water through its use in fertilizers and as a by-product of the burning of fuels such as gasoline. An excess of nitrogen upsets the biological balance of the entire planet. Chosen by *Time* magazine in 2001 as one of the United States's best scientists, Vitousek has used

u·x·l newsmakers • *volume 4*

his ground-breaking research in Hawaii to demonstrate the interconnectedness of ecosystems all over the world.

Childhood hobby becomes lifelong passion

Vitousek was born in 1949 in Honolulu, which is on Oahu, one of several islands that constitute the state of Hawaii. As a child, he was not especially interested in ecology or other environmental sciences, but he did enjoy spending time outdoors, exploring the island. He told *Environment Hawaii,* "[I] spent a lot of time hiking in the Ko'olau as a kid, not knowing what I was looking at very much, but liking being

> **"A tremendously important challenge is making people aware of just how extraordinary a place [Hawaii] is … not just for people in Hawaii appreciating what we have, but as an opportunity for people in the rest of the world to come and see and appreciate."**

outside a lot." His family spent part of each year in Kona, a coastal region on the island of Hawaii. Vitousek's father had grown up in that area, and his grandmother still lived there. During those trips to Kona, Vitousek spent time with some of his father's childhood friends, many of whom were ranchers and knew the land intimately. He learned a great deal about Hawaii's native vegetation and cultivated a love for his state's natural beauty.

When it came time to choosing a major in college, Vitousek chose a field that had little to do with his interest in exploring the outdoors. He began studying political science at Amherst College in western Massachusetts. He took an English course on the literature of science, a class that would alter his life's course. The class was assigned a book written by a British ecologist, Charles Elton, that detailed the impact of biological invasions. Sometimes, when a species of plant or wildlife is introduced to an area where that species does not ordinarily grow or live, it can take over, or invade, the area's ecosystem, having a tremendous and often damaging effect. The descriptions in Elton's book about the biological invasions in Hawaii ignited a spark in Vitousek. He recalled to *Environment Hawaii:* "A lot of things just came together for me then. I had that experience, seeing it and then reading about it and realizing that it fit somewhere in the context of conservation and of biology. I got really excited about doing something.…"

Vitousek began taking biology classes at Amherst. While he graduated in 1971 with a degree in political science, that subject had taken a back seat to other kinds of science in terms of his passion. After leaving Amherst, he enrolled in a postgraduate program at Dartmouth College, in Hanover, New Hampshire, earning his PhD in biological sciences there in 1975. Vitousek began his career teaching and conducting research at Indiana University and at the University of North Carolina. In 1984 he became a professor at Stanford University in Palo Alto, California. That university's location brought him closer to home, with Hawaii being just a few hours by plane from California. During the first few years he worked at Stanford, Vitousek spent more and more time conducting research in Hawaii. By the early 1990s, Vitousek was working almost exclusively in Hawaii, fulfilling his long-time goal of returning home. In 1990 he won a grant, known as a fellowship, from the Pew Fellows Program in Marine Conservation. This grant enabled him to study the effects of the introduction of nonnative grasses on Hawaii's local ecology. As part of his fellowship, he also helped to educate the public about environmental changes taking place around the world.

It's a small world after all

Based at the Hawaii Volcanoes National Park, Vitousek and his colleagues examine, as he told *Environment Hawaii,* "how whole ecosystems work, how the relationship between plants and soils works on large scales of space and time." Hawaii is an ideal testing ground for ecologists because it is so geographically isolated. Few species of plants occur naturally in Hawaii, and these few have had to adapt to the variety of climates and environments found there. Rather than trying to bring back to vitality areas that have been damaged, Vitousek's approach to protecting Hawaii's ecosystems consists of concentrating on the relatively unspoiled areas, working to keep these protected areas in the best shape possible. Such areas have been protected by organizations like the Nature Conservancy, which devotes itself to the preservation of plants and wildlife, as well as by national and state park systems. These areas have been saved from real estate development and have been monitored carefully to keep invasive species out and allow native species to thrive. "Those are places that are like no other places on earth," Vitousek told *Environment Hawaii.* "They are unique." Vitousek considers invasive species to be the greatest threat to ecosystems in Hawaii and elsewhere. *Time* magazine pointed out that such "biological invasions" have been responsible for tremendous ecological damage in Hawaii: "All of Hawaii's twenty species of flightless birds have vanished, and half the flying ones as well. One-sixth of the native plants are gone, and 30 percent of remaining ones are threatened."

One significant aspect of Vitousek's research has involved the study of how ecosystems thousands of miles apart can interact with and affect each other. He and his colleagues examined the chemical makeup of soil and rock at volcanic sites, which are abundant in Hawaii. Some of the sites were relatively young—just three hundred years old—and there, the plants derived their nutrients from the hardened lava. At the older sites, some as ancient as 4.1 million years, the scientists discovered that plants had been fed by minerals from another place entirely. The nutrients at these sites had arrived via ocean spray and dust, some of which had originated thousands of miles distant, in central Asia. Vitousek concluded, as he told *Time,* that "no ecosystem is entirely isolated."

Vitousek feels that one way to ensure that Hawaii's unspoiled areas are protected in the future is to educate people all over the world about what a special place Hawaii is. He told *Environment Hawaii,* "in terms of appreciating how the world works, evolutionarily, ecologically, culturally—there's nothing like Hawaii. And people who come here should see more of that, appreciate more of that, enjoy it more." Vitousek recognizes that many people think only of beautiful beaches and palm trees when they think of Hawaii, but he considers it vitally important to inform potential visitors that Hawaii has far more to offer. He wants to promote Hawaii as an ideal destination for eco-tourists, travelers who are passionate about visiting areas of extraordinary natural beauty. Vitousek understands that an increased number of tourists visiting Hawaii's remote, protected ecosystems could take a toll on those areas, but he feels the benefits outweigh the threats. As ever greater numbers of people come to feel as passionately as Vitousek does about preserving the world's natural treasures, the chances that such treasures will survive for generations to come increases tremendously.

Correcting an imbalance

In addition to finding ways to protect ecosystems, Vitousek has also focused his research on the issue of excess nitrogen in the environment. Nitrogen makes up 78 percent of Earth's atmosphere, but far more nitrogen than what naturally occurs has been found in water and soil throughout the world in recent decades. Some of the excess nitrogen is introduced through the burning of fossil fuels, which are extracted from the ground and come from the ancient remains of plants and animals. Fossil fuels include coal, natural gas, and crude oil. Crue oil is used to make gasoline and diesel fuel, which are burned by the engines of cars, trucks, and airplanes, among other machines. Another major source of excess nitrogen comes from fertilizers used in the growing of crops. Nitrogen is an essential nutrient for plants, and since the 1950s, farmers have increasingly used fertilizers that contain large quantities of synthetic, or human-made, nitrogen. While Vitousek recognizes that advancements in farming—including improvements made to nitrogen-containing fertilizers—have helped to feed billions of people, he asserts that the use of nitrogen should be carefully monitored to avoid upsetting the delicate balance of nature.

That balance has been disturbed by excess nitrogen. Nitrogen from fertilizers gets washed into rivers and lakes, eventually ending up in oceans and other large bodies of water. The presence of this nitrogen causes the explosive growth of certain types of algae, which are plants or plantlike organisms that grow in water. These algae "blooms" can be vast, and when they die, beginning to decay as they sink, they absorb oxygen in the water. The lack of oxygen then results in widespread suffocation among other marine plants and animals. Scientists have noted with great concern a large algae bloom—the size of the state of New Jersey—in the Gulf of Mexico. This bloom, believed to be the result of excess nitrogen, has been labeled a "dead zone" because of the inability of many species to survive in that area. The Gulf of Mexico dead zone is one of about fifty such areas in coastal waters worldwide. These dead zones have begun to pose a significant threat to marine ecosystems and, in some cases, have devastated a region's fishing industry.

Scientists have also noted a problem concerning nitrogen levels in soil. Some of the nitrogen released into the atmosphere from burning fossil fuels returns to the earth as part of acid rain, which is rain, snow, or fog that contains harmful levels of acid resulting from air pollution. When it becomes part of the soil, this type of nitrogen attracts important nutrients like potassium, magnesium, and calcium, taking those nutrients away from plants that need them. Excess nitrogen in the soil may lead to explosive growth among some plant species, but it can suffocate others.

Vitousek has worked to spread the word about the problems of excess nitrogen and the many harmful effects of this imbalance. He also educates people about what can be done to counteract this environmental problem. One way to improve the situation is more moderate use of nitrogen-based fertilizers on farms worldwide. Farmers can measure the amount of nitrogen in the soil and apply only as much fertilizer as absolutely necessary. In addition, farmers can plant more "nitrogen-fixing" plants such as soybeans, alfalfa, and peas, all of which are effective at converting the nitrogen that exists in the air into a usable nutrient, thereby reducing the need for fertilizers. Vitousek and many other environmental scientists also advocate a reduction in the burning of fossil fuels, which can be accomplished by the widespread use of more fuel-efficient cars. Vitousek has devoted his life to studying the inner workings of ecosystems and then applying his knowledge to recommend improvements in the global environment. Vitousek's colleague, Jane Lubchenco, a marine ecologist, told *Time* what makes the Hawaiian ecologist so unique: "Peter is a real visionary. It's unusual to have someone who is simultaneously interested in the big picture and in taking a very detailed look at the processes themselves."

For More Information

Periodicals

"Ecosystems Analyst." *Time* (August 20, 2001): p. 44.

Moffat, Anne Simon. "Ecology: Global Nitrogen Overload Problem Grows Critical." *Science* (February 13, 1998).

Nesmith, Jeff. "Nitrogen Used in Fertilizer Tips Delicate Balance." *Palm Beach (FL) Post* (November 3, 2002).

Web Sites

"An Interview with Peter Vitousek." *Environment Hawaii.* http://www.environment-hawaii.org/701an.htm (accessed on August 16, 2004).

"Pew Fellows." *Pew Fellows Program in Marine Conservation.* http://161.58.251.199/pewFellowsDirectoryTemplate.php?PEWSerialInt=3563 (accessed on August 16, 2004).

The White Stripes

Jack White

July 1975 • *Detroit, Michigan*

Guitarist, pianist, singer, songwriter

Meg White

c. 1974 • *Grosse Pointe, Michigan*

Drummer

Instantly recognizable in their stark red-and-white outfits, the White Stripes have become a worldwide phenomenon with their energetic blend of blues, punk, folk, and country. Consisting solely of Jack White on guitar and vocals and Meg White playing the drums, the Detroit-based White Stripes have been among the most visible groups connected to a revival of the loosely defined style known as garage rock—a usually fast-paced rock 'n' roll style favoring short songs with intense drumming and memorable lyrics. The White Stripes, however, bear the mark of a number of influences—not just the passionate, in-your-face Detroit signature sound they were raised with—including old-time country and traditional blues. With the release of their 2001 album *White Blood Cells,* the White Stripes graduated from regional success story to international stars. Their following release, *Elephant* (2003), further cemented their status, earning hordes of new fans, enthusiastic reviews from the music press, and a Grammy Award in 2004 for best alternative music album.

Even in the midst of tremendous recognition and fame, the group has insisted on maintaining a strong degree of independence and control, holding on to their unique vision. They tightly control how much and what kind of information the press receives about their personal lives, creating an aura of mystery. When they first began to receive national attention, Meg and Jack White told reporters that they were siblings. Later, it was revealed that their relationship was not one of brother and sister but rather ex–husband and wife. Even after proof of their relationship surfaced in the form of a marriage certificate and divorce documents, Jack White continued to insist, as he told *Entertainment Weekly*'s Tom Sinclair, that "we will

> "I consider everything about the songs—except the storytelling—to be a trick. If you're successful, and people love the songs, then you've successfully tricked them into liking the story."
>
> **Jack White, *Guitar Player*, June 2003.**

be brother and sister till the day we die." White additionally maintains control by producing every album the band makes. In an interview with *Guitar Player*'s Darrin Fox, White explained his reason for acting as producer: "I didn't want to argue with anybody about how we should sound. It's not an ego thing—I just wanted to be as in touch with the original idea as I could."

Meet the White Stripes

Born John Gillis, Jack White is one of ten children in a musical family raised in southwest Detroit. He started playing drums in elementary school. He first picked up one of his older brothers' guitars after receiving a reel-to-reel tape recorder. He started playing the guitar simply to record some basic tunes to accompany his drumming. Jack told Fox in the *Guitar Player* interview that he thinks starting as a drummer helped him become a better guitarist: "A lot of guitarists I respect, like Dick Dale, started off as drummers. I think it's interesting how rhythms are already in your head before you even know how to play guitar." He attended Cass Technical High School, also known as Cass Tech, a highly respected public school in downtown Detroit. As a teenager, Jack became intensely interested in the blues, delving into the music of such legendary artists as Blind Willie McTell, Robert Johnson, and Howlin' Wolf. While still in high school, he got a job working part-time at an upholstery company called Muldoon studio. He and the owner, Brian Muldoon, often jammed together, and Muldoon dipped into his extensive record collection to introduce White to the music of a number of influential bands. In 1994 Jack became the drummer for country-punk outfit Goober and the Peas.

In 1996 Jack and his girlfriend, Megan White, were married. Jack took his wife's surname, ever after being known as Jack White. The story of the band's origin involves Meg one day simply picking up drumsticks and playing along with Jack on guitar. "She was playing so childishly," Jack told Andrew Perry of *Mojo* magazine, intending the description as a compliment to Meg's simple, minimalist, untrained style. "So when Meg started playing that way, I was like, 'Man, don't even practice! This is perfect.'" Two months after Meg first picked up drumsticks, in 1997, the duo began playing gigs all over Detroit. They recorded two singles for the Detroit label Italy Records, "Let's Shake Hands" and "Lafayette Blues." They struggled for recognition, gradually winning over a small group of fans with Jack's songwriting and their passion for the music. During this time, Jack was invited to play guitar with the Detroit-based garage band the Go, an emerging band in the garage-rock scene. He joined the band, playing on their debut record. When the Go got a recording contract with the Seattle label (and former home to Nirvana) Sup Pop, Jack found himself at a crossroads. He felt that signing a contract with a band would compromise his freedom. He would not be the band's leader, and he knew that would not suit his personality. With the White Stripes, Jack would have the freedom to continually experiment, working in tandem with just one other performer: Meg. He left the Go and, by 1999, was completely focused on the White Stripes.

The White Stripes take off

The Stripes recorded their self-titled debut album in 1999. Made for about $2,000, the album was released by the independent Sympathy for the Record Industry label, located in California. The album, record-ed in part in the attic of Jack's parents' house, captured the raw, stripped-down power of the White Stripes' live show, but it also show-cased Jack's poetic, heartfelt lyrics. Writing for *All Music Guide,* Chris Handyside singled out the words to the White Stripes' songs, suggest-ing that it was the lyrics that set them apart: "The White Stripes are grounded in punk and blues, but the undercurrent to all of their work has been [a] striving for simplicity, a love of American folk music, and a careful approach to intriguing, emotional, and evocative lyrics not found anywhere else in … modern punk or garage rock." Looking back on their debut during a 2003 interview with *Guitar Player,* Jack White said, "I still feel we've never topped our first album. It's the most raw, the most powerful, and the most Detroit-sounding record we've made." In the fall of 1999, the White Stripes were invited to tour with Pavement and Sleater-Kinney, two bands that had earned critical praise and were fixtures of the independent-rock scene.

During the summer of 2000, not long after Jack and Meg White got divorced, the White Stripes released *De Stijl,* which means "the style." The title refers to an early twentieth-century art movement that emphasized simplicity and abstraction, or the depiction of objects in a way that makes them unrecognizable. Critics praised the White Stripes' second album for its primitive, basic style and the variety of songs, both originals and covers. In *Rollingstone.com* Jenny Eliscu described the album as "blues-tinged rock & roll scaled back to its most essential elements—one guitar, a simple drum kit, and sneering vocals." Heather Phares summed up *De Stijl* in *All Music Guide:* "As distinctive as it is diverse, *De Stijl* blends the Stripes' arty leanings with enough rock muscle to back up the band's ambitions."

Stars and Stripes

For their third release, *White Blood Cells* (2001), the White Stripes laid down some ground rules before recording began. First, they decided to avoid the genre they felt most passionate about: the blues. Jack explained to Fox in *Guitar Player* that he had always felt conflicted

about playing the blues, a genre that originated among African Americans in the South in the early twentieth century. Jack worried that fans might think his own interpretations of the blues—coming from a white man living in Detroit in the twenty-first century—were phony and inauthentic. So, as he told Fox, the White Stripes thought, "'What can we do if we completely ignore what we love the most?'" In addition to the "no blues" rule, they also, as Jack told Fox, "decided to record the album in three days, take no guitar solos, avoid slide guitar, and banish covers." The result was a CD featuring the Stripes' simple, tight arrangements and lyrics ranging from viciously angry to innocently sweet. *White Blood Cells* marked the band's arrival as an international favorite with both audiences and critics. The Stripes made the rounds on late-night talk shows, and their video for "Fell in Love with a Girl"—featuring animation of LEGO characters—went into heavy rotation on MTV. The video earned three MTV Video Music Awards (VMAs) in 2002. The album showed up on numerous critics' "top ten" lists for the year.

The Stripes continued their upward climb with their next album, *Elephant,* which was released in the spring of 2003. Heather Phares of

The White Stripes perform at the MTV Europe Music Awards in 2003. Kevin Mazur/WireImage.com.

All Music Guide wrote: *Elephant* overflows with quality—it's full of tight songwriting, sharp, witty lyrics, … judiciously used basses and tumbling keyboard melodies that enhance the band's powerful simplicity." The album showcases the female half of the duo more than previous releases had, with Meg contributing not just her telltale strong-but-simple drumming but also vocals on such songs as "In the Cold, Cold Night." Increasing numbers of critics and fans were won over by the Stripes' intensity and sincerity, somewhat unusual in an age where many artists feel that detachment is far cooler than passion. Writing in *Esquire,* Andy Langer expressed his appreciation for *Elephant:* "In the end, *Elephant* is an album destined for a long shelf life.… But its importance couldn't be any simpler or any more worth repeating: There are fourteen blistering songs on this record with Jack and Meg White's blood, sweat, and tears all over them. And every single one of them matters." The album certainly mattered to Grammy Award voters in 2004, who designated *Elephant* the best alternative music album of the previous year.

While keeping busy recording and touring with the Stripes, Jack White also tried his hand at acting with a small role in the 2003 film *Cold Mountain,* starring Nicole Kidman, Jude Law, and Renee Zellweger. He contributed several songs to the soundtrack. Most were covers of traditional songs, while one track, "Never Far Away," was composed by White. This soundtrack allowed White to further demonstrate his versatility and talent, prompting John Mulvey of *NME.com* to assert that "*Cold Mountain* proves what most of us have long suspected: when the White Stripes end, White will be far from finished."

Many fans of the White Stripes feel the band's power comes across best in live performances. Jack's guitars are old, inexpensive, beat-up instruments, and Meg's drum kit is small and simple. They rely very little on technology for their performances and recordings, instead banking on their energy, anger, and earnestness to carry their message forward. Jack told Fox in *Guitar Player:* "We put a lot of pressure on ourselves live. We don't have a set list, we don't rehearse, and we don't play the tunes exactly like on the album. We're just two people on stage with nothing to fall back on. But, that way, if something good comes out of it, we can really be proud because we know we did it for real."

For More Information

Periodicals

Fox, Darrin. "White Heat." *Guitar Player* (June 2003): p. 66.

Langer, Andy. "The White Stripes' *Elephant* Is a Rock 'n' Roll Record So Rousing, You Won't Mind Paying for It." *Esquire* (May 2003): p. 80.

McCollum, Brian. "A Definitive Oral History." *Detroit Free Press* (April 13, 2003).

Web Sites

The White Stripes. http://www.whitestripes.com/ (accessed on August 17, 2004).

"The White Stripes." *All Music Guide.* http://www.allmusic.com/ (accessed on August 17, 2004).

"The White Stripes." *Launch.* http://launch.yahoo.com/artist/default.asp?artistID=1042272 (accessed on August 17, 2004).

"White Stripes." *NME.com.* http://www.nme.com/artists/173888.htm (accessed on August 17, 2004).

"The White Stripes." *Rollingstone.com.* http://www.rollingstone.com (accessed on August 17, 2004).

Meg Whitman

1957 • ***Cold Spring Harbor, New York***

Chief executive officer

Meg Whitman is the president and chief executive officer (CEO) of eBay, Inc., the online auction site that became one of the World Wide Web's most surprising success stories. She took over the position from its founder, Pierre Omidyar, who remains active in the company, and has guided it into a commercial enterprise on a par with Amazon.com. Unlike other online sites, however, eBay enjoys impressive profits, thanks to its "virtual" presence. In essence, there is no warehouse, no sales staff, just a brand name and a collection of servers that connect buyers and sellers. In her posistion at eBay, Whitman is the first woman to become a billionaire thanks to stock holdings in an Internet company, and she freely admits that she learns as she goes. "Every week, there is a different set of issues, a different challenge, something new to think about," she told *Business Week* writer Robert D. Hof. "Probably at least a couple times a week, I go, 'Huh! I didn't know that.'"

Abandoned medical school dreams

Margaret "Meg" Whitman was born in 1957, the youngest of three children. She came from a well-to-do clan with ties to some of Boston's oldest families, and grew up in Cold Spring Harbor, a posh waterfront community in Long Island, New York. Her father, Hendricks, had his own loan business. Her mother, also named Margaret, was a homemaker, but when Whitman was in her teens her mother traveled to China as part of a women's delegation that had been invited for a visit. This was in the early 1970s, and the Asian nation had been closed to foreigners for many years until that point. Though Whitman was still in high school, her mother's achievement was an

> **"**We're a different company every three months. I ask myself from top to bottom, do we have the right people in the right place at the right time …? I even ask myself if I'm the right person for the right time.**"**

important part of her life. "When my mother came home after this great adventure," Whitman recalled in an interview with *Christian Science Monitor* journalist Patrick Dillon, "she told me what this experience taught her. She realized she could do anything she wanted and she wanted me to recognize that I could do the same."

Whitman was a talented athlete in high school, serving as captain of her swim team. She also played field hockey, lacrosse, and basketball. She entered Princeton University in 1973, just a few years after it began admitting undergraduate women for the first time. Planning on becoming a doctor, like many academic successes in high school she was tripped up by her organic chemistry class, among other courses. "I took calculus, chemistry, and physics my first year,"

Most Unusual eBay Sales

August 1999: Auction for human kidney reached a bid of $5.7 million before eBay removed it for violating sales policy.

2001: Gulfstream II jet sold for $4.9 million, thought to have been the most expensive item ever sold on the site.

June 2003: "Ghost in Jar" from Arkansas; winning bid: $50,922.

April 2004: Seattle man sells ex-wife's wedding dress after posting pictures of himself wearing it; winning bid: $ 3,850.

Other unusual auctions: lump of coal; piece of navel lint; a Lincoln Continental sedan once owned by President John F. Kennedy; boyhood home of former U.S. president Bill Clinton in Hope, Arkansas.

---

she explained to *Fast Company* writer Charles Fishman. "I survived. But I didn't enjoy it. Of course, chemistry, calculus, and physics have nothing to do with being a doctor, but if you're 17 years old, you think, This is what being a doctor is going to be about."

Whitman found her niche at college when she took an advertising sales job for a student magazine. She switched her major to economics, and after graduating from Princeton in 1977 went on to another Ivy League school, Harvard, where she earned a master's degree in business administration. In 1979 she was hired at Procter & Gamble, the Cincinnati, Ohio-based household and personal care products maker. One of her colleagues in the brand management department was Steve Case (1958–), who later founded America Online (AOL).

Married a doctor instead

While at Procter & Gamble, Whitman worked on the Noxzema skin care products team, but did not stay long at the company. She had married a Harvard medical student, Griffith Harsh IV, and because of his residency in neurosurgery, the couple had to relocate to San Francisco. There, Whitman found a job with Bain and Company, a global management consulting firm. She also became a mother during the 1980s, and her next job was a child's dream: that of senior vice president for marketing consumer products for Disney. She helped launch the company's new theme stores outside the United States, but began looking for a job in New England when her husband was offered the post of chief of neurosurgery at Massachusetts General Hospital in Boston. Fortunately, a shoe maker called Stride Rite in Lexington, Massachusetts, was looking for a new president.

During her time at Stride Rite, Whitman oversaw the revival of its vintage Keds sneaker line. Her next job was with Florists Transworld Delivery (FTD), a cooperative of florists, as president and chief executive officer, but she stayed only a year before going over to Hasbro, the toy maker. Not surprisingly, it was a decision that thrilled her young sons. Whitman ran Hasbro's preschool toys division, and successfully re-launched another vintage product, Mr. Potato Head.

In the fall of 1997 Whitman was contacted by a headhunting firm, which conducts searches for executives and other key corporate personnel. An online auction company was looking for a new leader to help launch it in earnest, but she had never heard of AuctionWeb, as eBay was still known. But Whitman agreed to fly to California for an interview. Before she left, she did some computer research on the company, when AuctionWeb was still a collection of classified ads. "I remember sitting at my computer saying, I can't believe I'm about to fly across the country to look at a black-and-white auction classified site," she recalled to Fishman.

Took risk at new company

EBay was still a relatively young company. It was started in 1995 in San Jose, California, by Omidyar, a computer programmer. He created the site and its software as a way to help his girlfriend sell items from her collection of kitschy Pez dispensers. The buy-and-sell by auction concept, in which the highest bidder wins, took off, and Omidyar's site turned a profit six months after it was launched. Its premise was simple: seller posts an item for sale and accepts auction bids over a two-week time frame. The highest bidder wins, and the buyer and seller exchange address information for payment and shipping. EBay charged a thirty-five-cent listing fee, and also took a small percentage of the sale transaction.

One of eBay's most important features was a rating system by which buyers and sellers rated their transactions with one another. Negative comments—about buyers who had not paid or sellers who had not shipped—would make others wary about doing business with either. Omidyar was convinced that listening and responding to the site's user base was crucial to his company's success. The online rating system itself had been suggested by eBay aficionados, for example. But he was having a difficult time expanding the company and maintaining his ethical outlook, and decided that a professional executive might do a better job in expanding eBay, as it had been renamed. Omidyar and the others in charge liked Whitman's customer service experience and brand management talents. She, in turn, liked eBay's sense of community spirit.

Whitman talked to her family, and they agreed to move. She started the job at eBay in February of 1998. The company had just nineteen employees at the time, and some were still using card tables as desks. Whitman delved in, taking a cubicle office like everyone else and even heading into fearsome high-tech territory. In June of 1999, with the company's site becoming more popular on a daily basis, its servers crashed for twenty-two hours. They had gone down before, but engineers had been able to find the problem quickly and fix it. This time was different. Whitman showed up at 4 A.M. and, as she told Atoosa Rubenstein in a *CosmoGirl!* interview, "moved in with the engineers for three months and effectively ran the technology division. I didn't know very much about technology, and it was a bit like being in France—everyone is speaking French, and I don't!"

An eBay "power seller" herself

Whitman also oversaw eBay's initial public offering (IPO) of stock in September of 1998, and over the next five years helped eBay become one of the most unusual success stories in American business history. It grew faster than Microsoft, Dell, Amazon, or Wal-Mart, and proved so successful for its sellers that many began quitting their day jobs in order to concentrate full-time on their online auctions. Heavy eBay pros were taking in $100,000 a year in sales, and some part-timers were helping to put their children through college with the extra income. EBay was said to have boosted the fortunes of an immense number of small specialty stores like antique shops and t-shirt makers, simply by giving their Web-savvy owners a whole new nationwide customer base.

Whitman instituted a policy at eBay that required its top executives to post items for auction regularly, so they would know firsthand

Margaret Whitman poses outside of eBay headquarters in San Jose, California. AP/Wide World Photo. Reproduced by permission.

what worked and what did not. She even sold the contents of her family's Telluride, Colorado, ski lodge. She also checked in regularly with the site's message boards to see what users were discussing. "The great thing about running this company," she told Brad Stone in *Newsweek,* "is that you know immediately what your customers think."

Under Whitman, eBay began holding annual member conferences for its top auctioneers. She is usually greeted like a rock star when she takes the stage, with the audience chanting her name. Honors have come from other sources, too: in 2002, *Fortune* magazine named her one of the three most powerful women in business. By then, eBay had over thirty million registered users, and took in $1.1 billion that year on a sales total that reached $15 billion in completed auctions. A year later that figure had risen to $24 billion in goods and services, and revenues had doubled to $2.17 billion. At any given time on eBay, about twenty million items are up for sale. Ten million bids are submitted by users every twenty-four hours, with $900 worth of goods and services exchanging hands every second.

Gave back to alma mater

Whitman has an annual salary of $2.19 million, but thanks to her ownership of eBay stock she is thought to be the first female billionaire created in the Internet age. She has donated some of her fortune to Princeton University, where she sits on the school's board of trustees. In early 2002 she and her husband donated $30 million to help the New Jersey school build a new residential college for undergraduates. Whitman College would be Princeton's sixth residential college, and would house about five hundred students. The added space would increase enrollment at Princeton from 4,600 to 5,100 when its first classes begin entering in 2010. "I had a great time as a Princeton undergraduate," a report in Ascribe Higher Education News Service quoted Whitman as saying, about her reasons behind the gift. "The University inspired me to think in ways that have guided me throughout my life."

Whitman works hard to balance her family life with a job she loves. She works out in the morning, and is usually able to drive her two sons to school. Vacations are often spent skiing or fly-fishing. When she travels for business, she rarely flies on the company plane. Thanks to the numerous business magazine covers that have featured her, fellow fliers recognize her and tell her their eBay stories. "I have one of the best jobs in Corporate America," she enthused to Hof. "It's this unique blend of commerce and community. The community of users is endlessly interesting and endlessly surprising. That's what I love the most."

For More Information

Periodicals

Bannan, Karen. "Sole Survivor." *Sales & Marketing Management* (July 2001): p. 36.

Dillon, Patrick. "Peerless Leader." *Christian Science Monitor* (March 10, 2004): p. 11.

Fishman, Charles. "Meg Whitman." *Fast Company* (May 2001): p. 72.

Hof, Robert D. "'The Constant Challenge' at eBay.' *Business Week* (June 30, 2004). This article can also be found online at http://www.business-week.com/technology/content/jun2004/tc20040630_3302_tc121.htm.

Hof, Rob. "Meet EBay's Auctioneer-in-Chief." *Business Week* (June 12, 2003). This articles can also be found online at http://www.business-week.com/technology/content/may2003/tc20030529_8665.htm.

Horsburgh, Susan. "EBay's eBoss." *People* (August 4, 2003): p. 97.

"Meg Muscles EBay Uptown." *Fortune* (July 5, 1999): p. 81.

"Meg Whitman to Support New Residential College at Princeton." Ascribe Higher Education News Service (February 4, 2002).

Stone, Brad. "Meg Gets on the Line." *Newsweek* (June 17, 2002): p. 56.

Rubenstein, Atoosa. "Team Player." *CosmoGirl!* (April 2003): p. 108.

Michelle Wie

October 11, 1989 • Honolulu, Hawaii

Golfer

Michelle Wie is a phenomenal, powerful golfer who regularly hits the ball nearly three hundred yards off the tee, about fifty yards farther than the average professional woman golfer. At nearly six feet tall and about 150 pounds, she has the strength and skills to match many professional players, including a number of men. In January of 2004 she competed in a men's event, the Sony Open, part of the Professional Golfers Association (PGA) tour. While she missed the second-round cut by just one stroke, she did end up beating forty-six men. During the summer of 2004 she was part of the U.S. team that won the prestigious Curtis Cup. In 2003 she won the U.S. Women's Amateur Public Links championship. While Wie has had a promising career so far, the reason for her headline-making status is not simply her accomplishments on the course: Wie is one of the most famous women golfers in the world because she became a world-class golfer before the age of fifteen. *Sports Illustrated*'s Michael Bamberger pinpointed the source of Wie's success in a 2003 article: "Her swing is a dream. No 150-

pound golfer, male or female, has ever made hitting a three-hundred-yard drive look so effortless."

Toddler golf

Michelle Sung Wie (pronounced WEE) was born in 1989 in Honolulu, a city on the island of Oahu, part of the state of Hawaii. She is the only child of Byung-Wook and Bo Wie, both of whom were born and raised in South Korea. Byung-Wook, known as B. J., acts as his daughter's coach; through 2003, he was her caddie as well. Aside from his coaching duties, he is a professor of transportation at the

---

"You can read about her all you want. You hear everything there is to be heard, but when you see her swing—when you see her hit a golf ball—there's nothing that prepares you for it. It's just the scariest thing you've ever seen."

Fred Couples, pro golfer and winner of 1992 Masters Tournament, in *Golf World* January 24, 2003.

University of Hawaii. Wie's mother, Bo, is a real estate agent and former Korean amateur champion golfer.

Wie began playing golf regularly at age four, at which point she could hit the ball one hundred yards. Her father told *Golf World*'s John Hawkins in 2003 that "Michelle has always liked to hit the ball hard. Sometimes it would go right, sometimes left, but it didn't matter. She just wanted to hit it hard." By age nine, having been coached by her father for many years, she was scoring better than her parents on the course. During 2000, at age ten, Wie became the youngest golfer to qualify for match play at a major adult event, the U.S. Women's Amateur Public Links (WAPL) championship, an extraordinary achievement that captured the attention of the media and golfing fans. By the time

Wie was twelve years old, she was winning most junior amateur tournaments, even the ones in which young men played as well. She stunned observers with her ability to drive the ball nearly three hundred yards, a distance many professional women golfers never achieve. After winning the Hawaii State Junior Golf Association's Tournament of Champions in 2001 and 2002, Wie and her parents felt that she could be a contender in major tournaments.

Playing in the big leagues

Early in 2002 Wie qualified for the Takefuji Classic, part of the Ladies Professional Golf Association (LPGA) tour. It was her first LPGA tour event, and while it is not a major tournament, Wie did make history by becoming the youngest golfer to qualify for

Michelle Wie watches her drive shot during the 2003 CJ Nine Bridges Classic in South Korea. AP/Wide World Photos. Reproduced by permission.

an LPGA event. In the 2002 WAPL, Wie reached the semifinals, again making history by becoming the youngest golfer to reach that level of competition. An accomplished student at Punahou School, a private academy in Honolulu, Wie began taking time out from her academics for intensive golf study in the spring of 2002, when she made her first visit to the David Leadbetter Golf Academy in Bradenton, Florida. She has since spent a great deal of time there, studying with Gary Gilchrist. Gilchrist has worked with a number of young women golfers, but he acknowledges that Wie possesses something unique. For a 2003 *Golf World* article he told Hawkins: "I don't know if we'll ever see a woman hit [the ball] this far with such effortless action. Ever."

In 2003, at age thirteen, Wie played in her first major event, the LPGA's Kraft Nabisco Championship at Rancho Mirage, California. She scored a stunning sixty-six in the third round, tying a record for the lowest score by an amateur at an LPGA major. She finished that round in third place, but her score of seventy-six in the final round resulted in a tie for a ninth-place finish. While her final score fell short of the promise exhibited in the third round, a top-ten finish for such a young player indicated the beginning of a stellar career. Later that year, Wie proved herself without a doubt: she won the WAPL championship, becoming the youngest player to win the event and indeed the youngest to win any adult United States Golf Association (USGA) event.

Success and controversy

In January of 2004, Wie demonstrated not just her skill but her courage and confidence by competing in a men's event: the Sony Open, run by the PGA, at Waialae Country Club in her home city, Honolulu. Her score after the initial two rounds was one stroke off from the cutoff, meaning that she did not advance to the third round. The youngest golfer ever to play in a PGA event, Wie tied for eightieth place overall, scoring higher than forty-six of her male competitors. While there is clearly room for improvement in her game, particularly her putting, some observers have described her swing as nearly perfect. Her caddie during the Sony Open, former South African professional player Bobby Verwey, told John Hawkins of *Golf World:* "That golf swing, it's the best I've ever seen. Everybody is looking for the perfect swing, but a twenty-five-year-old guy can't do that. The suppleness, the flexi-bility—you have to be fourteen to swing that way."

In March of 2004, Wie entered the Kraft Nabisco Championship for the second time, finishing in fourth place, up from her ninth-place finish the year prior. In June of 2004 she was part of the youngest squad in the history of the Curtis Cup, a prominent two-day event played every two years. No player on the U.S. team was over the age of twenty-five, and the team's average age was just a bit over eighteen. Wie was the youngest of the eight-member team by two years. Playing in northwest England, the U.S. team won the trophy, beating the Great Britain and Ireland team (GB&I), which had won the Curtis Cup every time since 1996. Wie's triumph at the Curtis Cup was followed by disappointment later that summer, when she tearfully lost the 2004 WAPL championship to another teenager, fifteen-year-old Ya-Ni Tseng from Taiwan. During that same summer, she played in a qualifying round for the U.S. Amateur Public Links championship, traditionally a men's event. She failed to qualify for the event, but she finished just two strokes behind the winners.

During a summer filled with competitive ups and downs, Wie found herself at the center of a controversy. On rare occasions, the USGA—which conducts thirteen national championships, both professional and amateur, each year—has offered exemptions to players in the Women's Open and the Men's Open, allowing those players to enter the tournament automatically without having to win qualifying rounds. Wie was granted a special exemption to play in the U.S.

Women's Open in July of 2004. When Wie's exemption was announced, many professional players expressed their disapproval. They felt that Wie should earn her way into the event, both for her own growth as a player and to be fair to other golfers. Many players agreed that the tour officials gave Wie the exemption because her presence at the Women's Open would attract more money from sponsors and from ticket buyers; opinions were divided over whether that financial motivation was good for the game of women's golf or not. Wie quieted many of her critics when she played well enough to make the cut after the second round, the point at which many players are eliminated. She finished the event in a tie for thirteenth place.

Hardly a normal life

Like many young golfers, Wie idolizes the game's top players, especially Tiger Woods and Ernie Els. Unlike most golfing kids, however, Wie had the opportunity to meet her idols, doing so during the 2004 Mercedes Championships, just before the Sony Open. Els and Woods generously gave Wie advice about her game and a boost in her confidence through their kindness and attention to her. Els invited Wie to join him in a practice round, offering putting pointers that significantly improved her performance. In a January of 2004 article in *Golf World*, John Hawkins wrote that Els "pulled the girl aside … and rebuilt her long-putting stroke in less than five minutes." Wie has even been granted a nickname—the Big Wiesy—that echoes that of Els, the Big Easy.

In spite of her early successes in events both amateur and professional, Wie does not plan to turn professional until after graduating from college. She hopes to attend Stanford University, the same college chosen by Tiger Woods. Once she turns professional, Wie's goals are simple but by no means easy: she plans to become a dominant player in both the LPGA and the PGA. As an amateur, she hopes to one day play in the Masters Tournament, golf's most prestigious event. The sticking point for women wishing to play in the Masters is that the event is held at Georgia's Augusta National Golf Club, a course no woman has ever played on.

As with other young elite athletes, Wie's early exposure to the intensity of high-level play and to media attention has caused many to express concern that she has forfeited her childhood and given up the chance at a normal life. Wie responded to such concerns in an interview with Tim Rosaforte of *Golf World:* "I guess I'm not normal, first of all, so I can't have a normal life. I guess if you grow up normal, you'll always be normal, and I don't want to be normal. I want to be something else."

For More Information

Periodicals

Bamberger, Michael. "Next Stop: U.S. Open." *Sports Illustrated* (July 7, 2003): p. 32.

Hawkins, John. "Island Girl." *Golf World* (January 24, 2003).

Hawkins, John. "Wie-markable." *Golf World* (January 23, 2004): p. 14.

Herrington, Ryan. "Old Enough for the Job." *Golf World* (June 18, 2004): p. 22.

Herrington, Ryan. "The Crying Game." *Golf World* (July 2, 2004): p. 21.

Rosaforte, Tim. "Youth Is Served." *Golf World* (June 27, 2003): p. 18.

Sirak, Ron. "Too Easy for Big Wiesy." *Golf World* (June 4, 2004): p. 5.

Web Sites

Kelley, Brent. "Michelle Wie Biography." *About.com.* http://golf.about.com/cs/womensgolf/a/wiequotes.htm (accessed on August 17, 2004).

"Meet Golf's Latest Teenage Sensation." *BBC Sport Academy.* http://news.bbc.co.uk/sportacademy/hi/sa/golf/features/newsid_2078000/2078650.stm (accessed on August 17, 2004).

"Michelle Wie: Pro Golfer." *Kidzworld.* http://www.kidzworld.com/site/p1848.htm (accessed on August 17, 2004).

Serena Williams

September 26, 1981 • Saginaw, Michigan

Tennis player

Beginning in the late 1990s, Serena Williams became one of the world's most talented and exciting tennis players. With her outgoing personality, unique fashion sense, and striking good looks, Williams would have commanded attention even if she hadn't been a top-ranked professional player. But her skills on the court happen to be extraordinary, the result of years of training, natural ability, and a powerful determination to win. Williams has gained additional attention as an African American athlete in a sport generally dominated by white players. Her 1999 singles victory at the U.S. Open made her only the second black woman ever to win a Grand Slam title; Althea Gibson (1927–2003) was the first. The Grand Slam tournaments—the Australian Open, Roland Garros (better known as the French Open), Wimbledon, and the U.S. Open—are among the game's most visible and significant events for pros.

By Williams's side—and often across the net—has been her older sister, Venus, an equally commanding player. Both sisters spent several years at the top of the world tennis rankings, each reaching the number-one position in 2002. As of the summer of 2004, Serena Williams had won six singles titles in Grand Slam events as well as numerous doubles titles, including a gold medal at the 2000 Olympic Games in Sydney, Australia. An ambitious, multitalented person, Williams has also, since 2002, explored acting, appearing in several television episodes and pursuing film roles as well. In addition, she has, along with her sister, studied fashion design.

From diapers to tennis skirts

The youngest of five daughters born to Richard and Oracene (who goes by the nickname Brandy), Serena and the rest of the Williams

> " Just watching her is inspiring. I just want her to have it all. To be honest, I want more for her than I do for myself. "
>
> Venus Williams, *People* magazine, June 28, 2004.

family moved from her birthplace of Saginaw, Michigan, to Compton, a suburb of Los Angeles, California, when she was a baby. An economically depressed area, Compton is a rough, often violent neighborhood, and the Williams sisters occasionally witnessed exchanges of gunfire. An avid fan of tennis, Richard Williams envisioned his daughters as champions even before they were born. He bought books and instructional videotapes, teaching himself and his wife how to play tennis so they could then teach their daughters. Both Serena and Venus showed promise at a very early age, prompting their outspoken father to begin making predictions about their future success in the tennis world. Coached by her father, Serena entered her first tennis tournament at age four and a half, and her father recalls that, over the next five years, she won forty-six of the next forty-nine tournaments she entered. She and Venus both excelled in the highly competitive preteen circuit in Southern California, both attaining a number-one

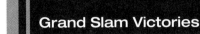

Grand Slam Victories

Serena Williams has won numerous singles and doubles titles at Grand Slam events (the Australian Open, the French Open, Wimbledon, and the U.S. Open). Below are listed her victories through the end of the 2003 season:

Singles:
Australian Open, 2003
French Open, 2002
Wimbledon, 2002, 2003
U.S. Open, 1999, 2002

Doubles (all with sister Venus):
Australian Open, 2001, 2003
French Open, 1999
Wimbledon, 2000, 2002
U.S. Open, 1999

Mixed Doubles (both with Max Mirnyi):
Wimbledon, 1998
U.S. Open, 1998

ranking in their respective age groups. Before reaching their teen years, the sisters had begun attracting attention far beyond the borders of their home state. They received offers for endorsement deals from sporting-goods companies and invitations to prestigious tennis camps.

In 1991 Richard Williams withdrew the girls from junior tournaments, a decision that was widely criticized by tennis insiders. The junior circuit is accepted as the conventional path to tennis stardom, but Richard wanted to protect his daughters from the intense competition and from what he perceived as racial hostility from other players. Richard invited teaching pro Rick Macci—who had earlier coached such tennis stars as Mary Pierce and Jennifer Capriati—to come to Compton and watch his daughters play tennis. Macci came, and he was impressed by the sisters' skill and athleticism. He invited them to study with him at his Florida academy, and soon after, the family relocated to the Sunshine State. The proceeds from a clothing endorsement contract for Serena and Venus allowed the family to purchase a home in Palm Beach Gardens, not far from the tennis school.

By 1993 the girls had left school, opting to continue their education at home and spend as much time as possible honing their tennis skills. Later they both returned to a school setting, enrolling at a small, private school called Driftwood Academy. Williams graduated from high school in 1999. In 1995, at age fourteen, Williams turned pro, arousing controversy among many who felt athletes should be older before they become professionals. The Women's Tennis Association (WTA), the governing body of women's professional tennis, barred competitors from WTA events at that age, so Williams's first pro event was a non-WTA tournament in Quebec, Canada. She was quickly eliminated from that competition. Her introduction to professional play indicated that she needed additional training time, and Richard decided that his youngest daughter should take a break from competition for the remainder of that year and the following year as well.

A tentative beginning

Williams began 1997, her first year as a WTA competitor, in the shadow of her sister, who had shown herself to be a promising young player. The Ameritech Cup in Chicago, however, made it clear that Serena Williams was more than just the little sister of Venus: she was a budding star in her own right. At that tournament, she shocked observers by defeating Mary Pierce, then ranked seventh in the world among women players, in the second round. Further defying expectations, Williams went on to defeat fourth-ranked Monica Seles in the quarterfinals before losing to Lindsay Davenport in the semifinals. She completed the 1997 season ranked ninety-nine, an impressive debut year for a sixteen-year-old player.

She continued to build her skills and confidence in 1998, beating a number of players ranked far above her. One such victory—beating ninth-ranked Irina Spirlea in the first round of the Australian Open—led her to a matchup against her sister in the next round. Venus won that match, a victory that aroused complex emotions for both sisters. Venus, accustomed to her role as big sister, wanted to take care of and protect her sister. Serena had spent most of her life looking up to Venus and working to be just like her. Both sisters, however, also felt an intense drive to win, regardless of who is on the other side of the net.

The Williams sisters have since met many times as opponents. Some observers have suggested that they lack their usual passion when they play each other, a charge both have denied. Such matchups do result in mixed feelings, however, with the victor feeling both triumphant and regretful. Serena and Venus are best friends, but they are also intensely competitive with each other, and each sister uses the other's success as motivation to improve. In a 1998 article, Serena told

Sports Illustrated for Kids, "I've learned a lot from watching Venus. Her results have encouraged me to work harder so that I can do well, too."

The Williams sisters have also played together many times as a doubles team, with 1998 marking the first time the sisters won a professional match together. Serena also won two Grand Slam mixed doubles titles that year—at Wimbledon and the U.S. Open—with partner Max Mirnyi. While she had yet to win a major singles title, Williams earned more than $2 million dollars during 1998. The following year proved even more successful, with Williams winning a number of events. Her first singles title of the year was at the Paris Indoors tournament; Venus won a tournament the same day in Oklahoma City, Oklahoma, marking the first time in the history of professional tennis that two sisters won championships on the same day—or even in the same week. The professional highlight of the year came when Williams defeated three of the top-four tennis players in the world to win the singles title at the U.S. Open. It was her first singles victory at a Grand Slam event, and the first time in more than forty years—since Althea Gibson's win in 1958—that an African American woman won a Grand Slam singles title. Another 1999 milestone was Williams's first professional victory over her sister, beating Venus in the Grand Slam Cup. The two teamed up to win two Grand Slam doubles events that year, at the French Open and the U.S. Open. Williams finished the 1999 season as the fourth-ranked women's player in the world.

Unstoppable

The following two years proved difficult for Williams, with a series of injuries resulting in a number of losses and forcing her to withdraw from several tournaments. High points of the 2000 season included doubles victories, with Venus as her partner, at both Wimbledon and the Olympic Games. The sisters won the doubles title at the Australian Open in 2001, marking their dominance in doubles at all four Grand Slam events.

Having recovered in spectacular fashion from her various injuries and illnesses of the preceding years, Williams seemed unstoppable in 2002. The best players in the women's game were no match for her unparalleled strength and speed on the court. She was victorious in eight out of the eleven tournaments she entered, earning nearly

$4 million in prize money. At the NASDAQ-100 Open in Miami, Florida, Williams defeated the top three players in the world, including her sister, to win the singles title. This achievement marked one of many history-making wins: she joined tennis great Steffi Graf (1969–) as the only ones to defeat the world's three best players in one tournament. Three times that year—at the French Open, Wimbledon, and the U.S. Open—Serena met Venus in the finals of a Grand Slam event, and three times she defeated her sister. After her victory at Wimbledon, Williams became the top-ranked women's tennis player in the world. During the U.S. Open Serena wore a one-piece black outfit made by Puma, a company she had signed a hefty endorsement deal with a few years earliers. The outfit—so different from the traditional white tennis dress—attracted nearly as much attention as Williams's playing. The real story of 2002, however, was that she was one of just seven women in the history of the game to win three consecutive Grand Slam titles in a single year.

Serena Williams holds up her championship Trophy at the 2002 U.S. Open. AP/Wide World Photos. Reproduced by permission.

The following year, 2003, Williams completed her sweep of Grand Slam events, beating her sister to win the singles title at the Australian Open. She won a number of other significant singles titles that year, including a second consecutive win at Wimbledon. She held on to her number-one ranking for over a year, until August of 2003. Williams's extraordinary success was recognized by the cable sports network ESPN during its annual ESPY awards program: she won the ESPY for best female tennis player and best female athlete. The year proved a difficult one regarding injuries, but such problems seemed insignificant compared to the tragedy Williams and her family endured in September of 2003: her sister, Yetunde Price, was killed in Los Angeles, a victim of a random act of violence.

Life outside of tennis

For much of 2004, Williams dealt with a recurring knee injury. She won the NASDAQ-100 Open in Miami for the third year in a row, but at many other tournaments of the year she was either defeated or had to withdraw due to injury. Her pursuits outside of tennis began taking up more of her time as well, particularly her efforts to become an actress. Beginning in 2002, Williams started earning guest roles on various television shows, including *My Wife and Kids,* Showtime's *Street Time,* and *Law and Order.* She also scored a part in *Hair Show,* a feature film completed in 2004. Williams told Alex Tresniowski of *People* magazine that she's a natural-born performer: "If I hadn't played tennis, I was destined to be an actress. I'm a complete drama queen."

Williams has, in spite of her tremendous wealth and success, remained down to earth. She is a devout Jehovah's Witness, a Christian denomination that involves intensive Bible study and the preaching of biblical teachings to others. While some have criticized the Williams sisters for what they perceive to be arrogance and unfriendliness, Serena and Venus have also developed a reputation for avoiding petty exchanges of insults among tennis players. As world-famous tennis stars, they have been the subject of numerous rumors and negative reports in the media, but they try to ignore such press. In an interview with Oprah Winfrey for *O, The Oprah Magazine,* Serena reported that she doesn't care what others think of her—"as long as my family knows who I am. And I know that a lie can't live forever. Most of the lies people tell about us are eventually washed away, so they don't bother me." Williams attributes her levelheadedness to her strong family relationships and spiritual background. "My mom raised us to be strong women," she told Winfrey. "We were taught that things like peer pressure didn't exist for us."

For More Information

Periodicals

Leand, Andrea. "Smash Sisters." *Sports Illustrated for Kids* (August 1998): p. 34.

Toure. "The Queen." *Sports Illustrated Women* (December 1, 2002): p. 62.

Tresniowski, Alex. "Second Serve." *People* (June 28, 2004): p. 136.

Winfrey, Oprah. "Oprah Talks to Venus and Serena Williams." *O, The Oprah Magazine* (March 2003): p. 186.

Web Sites

Serena Williams. http://www.serenawilliams.com/ (accessed on August 17, 2004).

"Serena Williams." *ESPN.com.* http://espn.go.com/tennis/s/wta/profiles/ swilliams.html (accessed on August 17, 2004).

"Serena Williams." *WTA Tour.* http://www.wtatour.com/players/player profiles/PlayerBio.asp?ID=&EntityID=1&CustomerID=0&OrderID=0 &ReturnURL=/&PlayerID=230234 (accessed on August 24, 2004).

Yao Ming

© Duomo/Corbis.

September 12, 1980 • Shanghai, China

Basketball player

Yao Ming of China became basketball's most unlikely new celebrity athlete in 2002 when he joined the Houston Rockets. The first foreign athlete ever to become a number-one draft pick in the National Basketball League (NBA), Yao stands seven-foot, five inches tall, and proved to be a surprisingly quick and graceful player during his rookie season. He is a favorite among fans and sportswriters, coming across as humble, modest, and immensely likable. He is also the first Chinese athlete to attain international celebrity status.

Reached adult height by third grade

The future NBA star was born on September 12, 1980, in Shanghai, the largest city in China. Yao is his family's name, and Ming his given name. At birth, he weighed ten pounds and was the only child of parents who were unusually tall themselves. His father, Yao Zhiyuan, stands six-foot, ten inches tall, and was a basketball player for a local

Shanghai team. Yao's mother, Fang Fengdi, was six-foot, two inches in height and had played on the Chinese national team in the early 1970s.

Yao grew rapidly as a child. Because China had historically struggled to feed its population of 1.3 billion, city dwellers sometimes had to use ration coupons to buy food. For Yao's family, it seemed there was never enough food to satisfy the young boy's appetite, and his mother would visit the stalls of the city's food market near closing time to buy extra items cheaply. By the time he was in the third grade, he was five-foot, seven inches tall. Local sports officials took notice, and he was chosen to take part in a local sports school in Shanghai.

> "I want people in China to know that part of why I play basketball is simply personal. In the eyes of Americans, if I fail then I fail. It's just me. But for the Chinese if I fail then that means that thousands of other people fail along with me. They feel as if I'm representing them."

At first Yao was not overly interested in basketball or in any other sport. Instead, he liked books about military history, and could recite details of ancient battles from China's past. When he reached the sixth grade he was taller than his mother, and three years later had reached his father's impressive height. That same year, when he was in the ninth grade, he was signed to a contract with a Shanghai youth team. At the age of seventeen, he became the Shanghai Sharks' star player during its first full season.

The Sharks belonged to the Chinese Basketball Association (CBA), a government-controlled national league. Though soccer was still China's most popular spectator sport, basketball had grown increasingly popular during the 1990s. Soon there were more partici-pants in basketball programs than there were playing soccer in China,

The NBA's New International Flavor

Yao Ming was one of several new foreign players signed to American teams in the 2002 NBA draft. Though he was the first to become a number one draft pick, Yao joined a roster of players that included Luis Scola from Argentina, Bostjan Nachbar from Slovenia, and Brazilian star Maybyner "Nene" Hilario. Of the fifty-seven players drafted, sixteen were from overseas teams, a league record.

Some thirty-four nations are represented in the NBA player roster. One of the first foreign stars was Manute Bol, a seven-foot, seven-inch Sudanese player in the 1980s. The increasing number of athletes from Europe, Africa, and now even Asia comes thanks to interest in the sport in faraway places. Interest in the NBA teams grew with the help of satellite television, which broadcast NBA games, and when the league began taking top players on overseas exhibition tours.

In countries outside of the United States, the college athletic tradition is virtually nonexistent. Sports facilities exist solely for training national athletes for the Olympics. Professional sports is dominated by soccer, with intense national rivalries, players who become household names, and sold-out stadiums in every city. But professional basketball teams have also gained a foothold in European cities. Talented players, both homegrown and imported, can join teams and turn professional when they are still in their teens. They gain valuable competitive experience which makes them ready to play in the NBA.

Still, there is some criticism of the new face of the NBA, and hints that the new emphasis on foreign players may be a backlash against the "bad boy" reputation of some of its biggest stars, like Dennis Rodman, Charles Barkley, and Kobe Bryant. As *Village Voice* writer Dan McGraw explained: "The perception—and perception is always important in matters of race—is that the NBA is acing out the black man because of corporate (read: white) fans and international marketing money. High-scoring white guys equals big bucks."

In June of 2004, Ha Seung-Jin became the NBA's first Korean player. Drafted by the Portland Trail Blazers, the seven-foot, three-inch player has been hailed as the next Yao Ming. His Asian fans have dubbed him "Ha-Quille O'Neal.' But Ha hopes to follow Yao's example, telling Peter Hessler of the *New Yorker,* "I want to be a Korean Yao Ming."

and NBA games broadcast on state-run television attracted large audiences. Yao was also a member of the Chinese national team, which competes in international events like the Olympics.

Visited America in 1998

Yao's immense height and court skills began attracting notice outside of China. Player scouts for NBA teams had discovered him, and so had sports marketing companies. In 1998 the athletic gear maker Nike invited him to the United States for a series of basketball camps. It was an important milestone for Yao, as he told Peter Hessler in a profile that appeared in the *New Yorker.* "Before then, I was always playing with people who were two or three years older than me," he explained. "They were always more developed, and I didn't think that I was any good. But in America I finally played against people my own age, and I realized that I was actually very good. That gave me a lot of confidence."

For the next few years, Yao was caught between his country and the chance to become an international superstar. China wanted to keep him with the Sharks and on the national team, and was not eager to see him leave the country for a million-dollar contract to play with the NBA. A sports marketing firm almost engineered a deal in 1999, but it involved giving the Sharks a large percentage of his potential American paycheck, which would have been prohibited by NBA players' union rules. In the spring of 2000, Yao was invited to the Nike Hoop Summit—where many international players show off their talents before NBA scouts—but the Chinese government refused to let him go. The Chinese national team was about to begin its Olympic workouts, the official explanation went, and wanted Yao to be prepared for the 2000 Summer Games in Sydney, Australia.

Yao and his national teammates made an impression in Sydney. He played alongside six-foot, eleven-inch Beijing Ducks player Menk Batere and Wang Zhizhi, a seven-foot, one-inch standout on the Chinese Army team. They were dubbed the "Walking Wall of China" for their prowess, but China was defeated by an all-star U.S. team, 119–72. Wang went on to become the first player from China to enter the NBA draft in 2001, and Batere was also signed that year by the Denver Nuggets, but Yao remained in China. One of the reasons may have been his age: if a player has not come up through the college ranks, he must be twenty-two years old to play in the NBA when his rookie season kicks off.

Joined Rockets in 2002

Yao continued to play for the Sharks, where he earned about $20,000 a year, leading them to the CBA championship in 2002. During one of the playoff games, Yao he took twenty-one shots and sank every one of them. Finally, terms were hammered out between NBA and CBA

Yao Ming of the Houston Rockets shoots over Amare Stoudemire (bottom) during a 2003 game against the Phoenix Suns. AP/Wide World Photos. Reproduced by permission.

officials that allowed Yao to enter the 2002 NBA draft. The CBA agreed to release him from his contract in exchange for a small percentage of his NBA salary. When the Houston Rockets won the draft-pick lottery that gave them first dibs, Yao was their first choice as a center. He was signed to a four-year, $18 million contract, with five percent of his salary going to the CBA. He was also the first number one draft pick to come from the international players' ranks.

The NBA's newest player attracted immense media attention, but Yao had to give most of his press interviews through a translator at first. He did not start for the Rockets during the first months of his rookie season, but began to show impressive talents whenever coach Rudy Tomjanovich put him in a game. On November 17, 2002, in a match against the Los Angeles Lakers, Yao scored twenty points for his team and made all of the shots he attempted—nine for nine. A few games later, he scored thirty points in a game against the Dallas Mavericks and took sixteen rebounds. In December he was named the Western Conference's rookie of the month.

Several weeks later, Yao made it onto the NBA All-Star team, beating out Shaquille O'Neal of the Lakers in fan voting for the best center. Relations between the two players had been slightly strained when Yao first came to the United States, because sportswriters liked to ask O'Neal, the NBA's most famous center, what he thought of his new competition. At one point, O'Neal made a disparaging remark in which he mimicked the Chinese language. In response, Yao reacted gracefully. "Chinese is hard to learn," he told one journalist when asked what he thought about the "Shaq" attack, according to Hessler. "I had trouble with it when I was little."

Dubbed basketball's "Gentle Giant"

With his own English-language skills improving, Yao began speaking to the media on his own more frequently. He quickly emerged as a fan favorite in Houston. During his rookie season, ticket sales for home games at Compaq Center jumped to about two thousand more than the previous year's figures. His nice-guy attitude and easy smile, combined with his immense height and lantern jaw, prompted the press to nickname him the "Gentle Giant." Corporate America was eager to hire him, too, and he was signed to a number of advertising contracts. In one of his first, which required no dialogue, he appeared alongside Verne "Mini Me" Troyer from the *Austin Powers* movies in an ad for Apple Computer. He also starred in a Visa check card commercial. Reebok signed him to an endorsement contract rumored to be $100 million dollars, thought to be the largest ever between a shoe company and an athlete.

Yao was an even bigger celebrity in China now. He pitched the Yanjing brand of beer, made in Beijing, and appeared in television commercials for China Unicom, a telecommunications company. In 2003 he returned home to play on the Chinese national team, and also hosted a multi-national telethon that raised money for SARS (Severe

Acute Respiratory Syndrome) awareness and prevention. Back in Houston, Yao had another excellent season with the Rockets in 2003, averaging 17.5 points and nine rebounds per game. In one match against the Atlanta Hawks in February of 2004, Yao scored a career-high forty-one points. More important, he helped take the Rockets to the NBA playoffs, but they lost the series to the Los Angeles Lakers.

Yao is well-liked by his teammates, even though his stardom could have brought bad feelings. They call him "Dynasty," a reference to the Ming era of Chinese history. His impressive court skills certainly help. Yao's former Rockets teammate Moochie Norris told one journalist that "when he throws you a pass, a lot of times he has to shout out your name so you know it's coming," the New York Knicks guard told Sean Deveney of the *Sporting News*.

Dwarfed Olympic team delegation

Yao still played for the Chinese national team. At the opening ceremonies of the 2004 Summer Games in Athens, Greece, he carried the Chinese flag when his country's Olympic delegation marched into the stadium. Once again he was the tallest athlete at the Olympics. In the NBA, only seven-foot, six-inch Shawn Bradley of the Dallas Mavericks is taller than Yao. In China, broadcasts of Rockets' games on television draw fourteen million viewers, and Yao is mobbed by fans whenever he returns. One Chinese man, Zhang Guojun, explained to a journalist why China's most famous athletic is such a beloved figure. "Yao is important in our hearts," he told Hessler. "He went to America, and he returned."

Yao lives near Katy, Texas, in a home he shares with his parents. Though he is surprised at the media attention his NBA career has brought, he says he always hoped to achieve greatness in his profession. "When I was small, I always wanted to be famous," he confessed to Hessler. "I thought I'd be a scientist or maybe a political figure. It didn't matter, as long as I was famous."

For More Information

Periodicals

Beech, Hannah. "Yao Ming: China's Incredible Hulk of the Hardcourt Becomes an NBA Sensation." *Time International* (April 28, 2003): p. 34.

Deveney, Sean. "Bigger and Better." *Sporting News* (January 20, 2003): p. 6.

Hessler, Peter. "Home and Away." *New Yorker* (December 1, 2003): p. 65.

Larmer, Brook. "Dreams Deferred." *Newsweek International* (April 10, 2000): p. 69.

McCallum, Jack. "Sky Rocket." *Sports Illustrated* (February 10, 2003): p. 34.

McGraw, Dan. "The Foreign Invasion of the American Game." *Village Voice* (May 28, 2003). This article can also be found online at http://www.villagevoice.com/issues/0322/mcgraw.php.

Murphy, Michael. "NBA Draft: These Guys Are World Beaters." *Houston Chronicle* (June 27, 2002): p. 6.

Rodgers, Marshall. "The Tao of Yao." *Basketball Digest* (May 2003): p. 46.

Web Sites

"Yao Ming." *NBA.com.* http://www.nba.com/playerfile/yao_ming/bio.html (accessed on August 9, 2004).

José Luis Rodríguez Zapatero

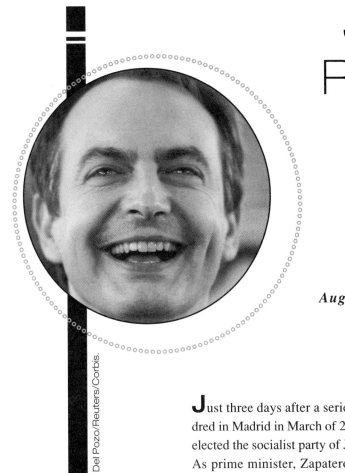

© Marcelo Del Pozo/Reuters/Corbis.

August 4, 1960 • *Valladolid, Spain*

Prime minister

Just three days after a series of bomb blasts killed nearly two hundred in Madrid in March of 2004, Spanish voters went to the polls and elected the socialist party of José Luis Rodríguez Zapatero into office. As prime minister, Zapatero promised to withdraw Spanish forces from Iraq, and ordered those troops home just hours after he was sworn in four weeks later. His party's victory was widely seen as a rejection of the pro-American policies of his predecessor, José María Aznar and his Popular Party (PP).

Came from renowned liberal family

Zapatero was born in 1960 in the city of Valladolid, north of Madrid. His family were of Castilian background and were originally from the city of León. His father was an attorney; his grandfather had been killed during the Spanish Civil War of the 1930s. Spain had established a republic in 1931, with the king abdicating his throne, but civil

unrest continued, and reached a crisis point by 1936. A military officer, Francisco Franco, attempted a coup, and a bloody war ensued.
Zapatero's grandfather, who fought on the Republican side, was slain
by Franco's soldiers during the first weeks of the war.

Franco and his Nationalists ultimately won the war and installed
a military dictatorship that endured until Franco's death in 1976. Zapatero was sixteen years old at the time. He attended his first political
meeting just a few weeks later, in August of 1976, although political
parties were still technically illegal. At that rally, he was impressed by
a speaker, future prime minister Felipe González, and joined
González's Spanish Socialist Workers' Party, or PSOE, two years

"My most immediate priority is to beat all forms of terrorism."

later. Zapatero went on to study law, and taught the subject at León
University from 1982 to 1986. At the lectern, he specialized in Spanish constitutional law, a relatively new field with Spain's constitution
in place only since 1978.

Zapatero also became a rising star in the PSOE. He headed the
party's youth organization in León, and in 1986, when he was just
twenty-six years old, became the youngest member of parliament
when he was elected from the province of León on the PSOE ticket.
The PSOE dominated Spain's post-Franco political era. González,
head of the party, became prime minister in 1982, and held the post for
the next fourteen years. Corruption scandals, however, blackened the
party's reputation in the early 1990s. In response, Spanish voters elected the center-right Popular Party (PP) of José María Aznar in 1996.

Rose to party leadership post

By 1988 Zapatero had been elected secretary-general of the PSOE
chapter in León province. Over the next decade he worked to reform
the party from inside, as a response to the corruption scandals. He and

Spain's Basque Problem

Terrorist threats were already a fact of life for Spaniards long before a series of bombs in backpacks went off in Madrid on March 11, 2004. Since the 1960s a Basque group, Euskadi Ta Askatasuna (ETA), had carried out similar acts in order to gain support for their goal of political sovereignty.

The Basques number nearly three million, but not all of them live in Spain. Some reside in mountain villages just across Spain's border with France in the Pyrenees. Their language, Euskara, is different from any other language in the world. Linguists believe it may have origins in the Sino-Tibetan language family, or is connected with the Berber language of North Africa.

The origins of the Basque people have been one of Europe's greatest mysteries. They may have come to Europe with the Indo-European migration that occurred around 2000 B.C.E. Another theory claims they were settled in the Iberian peninsula (Spain and Portugal) long before, when Cro-Magnon man became dominant in Europe. This would make them Europe's oldest surviving ethnic group. They survived the Roman Empire invasions, and ambushed and massacred Charlemagne's troops in 778 C.E. in what is known as the Battle of Roncevaux Pass.

For centuries the Basques remained isolated and self-sufficient, weathering the Moorish Islamic invasion of the Iberian peninsula as well as a series of successive kingdoms that dominated Spain. They converted to Christianity, but may have been sun-worshippers in earlier times. Renowned fishers, they became major suppliers of cod to the rest of Europe, but where they found their fish remained a mystery for hundreds of years. Then, in the 1530s, French explorer Jacques Cartier arrived at the mouth of the St. Lawrence River in Canada and reported thousands of Basque fishing boats already there.

The Basques managed to maintain much of their unique identity for generations. They were nominally allied with the Spanish monarchy, but had their own set of laws, called *fueros*. Their independence was eroded after the terms of deals made during Spain's contentious internal wars during the nineteenth century were not honored. During the Spanish Civil War of the 1930s they surrendered to Italian troops, and Spain's victorious military dictator, Francisco Franco, removed nearly all of their autonomy.

Out of that grew the ETA, a guerrilla group formed in 1959. It carried out its first attack, a train derailment, two years later. The first death from an ETA act came in 1968. In 1973 ETA operatives assassinated the Spanish prime minister, Admiral Luis Carrero Blanco. Over the next three decades, the ETA planted car bombs and devices on trains, but a crackdown limited much of their power by 2003, when a train-station attack on Christmas Eve was successfully thwarted by the government's anti-terrorism squad. Few thought the ETA was repsonsible for the Atocha attacks in March of the following year, since the group almost always alerted authorities to a bomb they had planted.

a coalition of other like-minded PSOE politicians urged a modernization of the party's platform, modeling it after Tony Blair's remake of the Labour Party in the mid-1990s. The reform movement gained momentum, but the PSOE failed to beat Aznar's party in national elections held in March of 2000. The head of the PSOE at the time,

Joaquín Almunia, resigned as a result of the poor showing, and at the next party conference that July, PSOE delegates elected Zapatero as their new national secretary-general. Elizabeth Nash, a writer for London's *Independent* newspaper, quoted Zapatero as saying he would personally "lead this party once more to victory and the biggest one in its history." He added, "We need change, tranquil change. Our hope is for victory in 2004."

Zapatero began to take steps to win over Spanish voters to his party. In the fall of 2000, Zapatero and Aznar forged an agreement that their parties would work together to eliminate the threat of home-grown terrorists, which had been a serious concern in Spain for a number of years. A separatist movement in the north of Spain, Euskadi Ta Askatasuna (ETA), translated as "Basque Fatherland and Liberty," had emerged in the 1960s, and called attention to its cause through bombings and assasinations. More than eight hundred Spaniards had died since then. Zapatero and Aznar pledged that they would not allow the ETA threat to be used for the political gain of their own parties, and pledged to work together to end the bloodshed. They even led a march through the streets of Barcelona against ETA terrorism that November.

The renewed effort against the ETA seemed to work, and many arrests were made. At the same time, Aznar's PP government was proving increasingly unpopular. It was criticized for its handling of an oil tanker spill off Spain's northern coastline in Galicia in November of 2002, which paralyzed the region's fishing industry for months. It was later revealed that Aznar's government had initially underreported the scope of the environmental disaster. In May of 2003 an aging military transport plane carrying Spanish troops back from Afghanistan crashed in Turkey, killing sixty-two. Protesters called for the resignation of Aznar's minister of defense, saying the Soviet-made, Soviet-era planes were known to have been unsafe.

Opposed war in Iraq

Aznar's most serious political error, however, seemed to be his support of U.S. President George W. Bush in the latter's effort to oust Iraqi leader Saddam Hussein in 2003. Aznar's decision to send a small contingent of Spanish troops to join the coalition forces that invaded

Iraq was met with a public outcry; opinion polls showed that seventy percent of Spaniards opposed the war. Zapatero took a strong stance against the war. As PSOE head, Zapatero rejected any alliance with America, although Aznar had tried to persuade him to give his support in the interests of national unity. After meeting with Aznar, Zapatero appeared at a press conference and told journalists that he refused to comply with Aznar's plea. "I told him the Socialist Party does not support a preventive attack on Iraq," *New York Times* writer Emma Daly quoted him as saying, "because there are no causes and reasons to justify an action of this magnitude."

In the run-up to the 2004 national elections, one of Zapatero's first campaign promises had been a pledge to withdraw the 1,300 Spanish troops in Iraq if elected. "This government doesn't serve Spaniards anymore, it only serves the interests of Bush," *New York Times* writer Lizette Alvarez quoted him as saying. As the election season moved into full swing, many were surprised at Zapatero's new fierceness on the campaign trail, as he condemned Aznar's government in the strongest terms. In past years, newspaper editorial cartoonists had sometimes poked fun of Zapatero as *Sosoman,* or "Dullman," depicting him wearing a superhero costume.

The Madrid bombings, thought to have been timed to disrupt the Spanish elections, seemed to be the decisive factor in the PSOE victory at the polls. On March 11, a series of bombs went off at Madrid's main train station and on trains elsewhere in the city during the morning rush hour. The catastrophe, the deadliest attack on European soil since World War II, left 192 dead and more than 1,400 injured. The Aznar government initially blamed it on ETA terrorists, but evidence began to mount that the attack might have been carried out by al-Qaeda—the terrorist group responsible for the September 11, 2001, attacks in the United States—operatives in Spain. Spaniards who were opposed to the war in Iraq noted that Aznar's decision to side with the Bush White House had made Spain vulnerable to such attacks. They took to the streets by the thousands to mourn the dead and voice their opposition to government policy as well. Despite evidence pointing to al-Qaeda, the Aznar government continued to insist that ETA had been responsible, which was widely viewed as a political ploy to forestall a loss at the polls that weekend.

José Luis Rodríguez Zapatero (left) is sworn in as the Prime Minister of Spain, April 17, 2004. Onlookers include Spanish King Juan Carlos (right) and Queen Sofia. © Reuters/Corbis.

Recalled troops from Iraq

Three days later, on Sunday, a record voter turnout ousted Aznar's party and his handpicked successor, Mariano Rajoy, in favor of Zapatero and the PSOE. Even Rajoy was jeered by protesters when he cast his own ballot at a Madrid polling station. In the official tally the Popular Party won 38 percent of the vote, but Zapatero's socialists took 43 percent of the vote and 164 seats out of the 350 in the Cortes, the lower house of parliament. The PSOE won 29 seats more than it had in the previous election.

Just days after the election, a leading newspaper in Spain, *El Pais,* published an interview with Zapatero. "The war in Iraq was a huge mistake," he asserted, according to an article by *New York Times* correspondent Elaine Sciolino. "There was no motive. It was done without international consensus, and the management of the occupation has been a disaster." For his cabinet, Spain's new prime minister named a respected diplomat, Miguel Angel Moratinos, to be his foreign minister. Moratinos was a veteran of Middle Eastern diplomacy issues, and had previously served as Spain's ambassador to Israel.

Zapatero was sworn into office on April 17, 2004, by King Juan Carlos at Madrid's Zarzuela Palace. Twenty-four hours later, he made the announcement that he had ordered all 1,300 Spanish troops in Iraq to return home as soon as possible. During his first year in office, he also proved to be a liberal on domestic matters. He pledged to create new policies that would grant same-sex couples in Spain the same legal rights as married heterosexuals. A year earlier, the Cortes had passed a new law, amidst great controversy, that forced all public schools in Spain to make religious instruction a part of the curriculum. Zapatero announced that his government would not allow the law to go into effect. Furthermore, he vowed to eliminate gender bias in Spain via a sweeping series of new laws.

Zapatero's wife, Sonsoles Espinosa, maintains a low profile and rarely appears by his side. She is a voice teacher and shuns the political spotlight. The couple have two daughters.

For More Information

Periodicals

Alvarez, Lizette. "In His Startling Leap to High Office, Socialist Takes Strong Stand Against 'an Unjust War.'" *New York Times* (March 15, 2004): p. A12.

Daly, Emma. "Spain's Chief, on Bush's Side, Comes Under Attack at Home." *New York Times* (February 4, 2003): p. A12.

Graff, James. "Getting to the Truce." *Time International* (April 26, 2004): p. 35.

"Jose Luis Rodriguez Zapatero, Spain's New Socialist." *Economist* (January 27, 2001): p. 8.

Nash, Elizabeth. "Madrid: The Aftermath: How the Quiet Man of Spanish Politics Finally Made His Voice Heard Above the Noise of War." *Independent* (London, England), (March 16, 2004): p. 6.

Sciolino, Elaine. "A New Future for Spain: Call It Social Socialism." *New York Times* (March 31, 2004): p. A4.

Sciolino, Elaine. "Spain's New Leader Blows Both Hot and Cold Toward U.S." *New York Times* (March 22, 2004): p. A3.

Sharrock, David. "Quiet Man Who Swept to Power on a Wave of Anger." *Times* (London, England) (March 16, 2004): p. 16.

Volume numbers are in italic; **boldface** *indicates main entries and their page numbers; (ill.) following a page number indicates an illustration on the page.*

Cheeba, Eddie, *4:* 701

Cheetah Girls, The, 3: 619

Chen, Christine Y., *3:* 610

Cheney, Sarah Haddad, *3:* 453, 454

Cher, *2:* 407

Chess (play), *2:* 309

Chestnut, Morris, *4:* 779

Chestnut Soldier, The (Nimmo), *3:* 507, 508

Chicago (Broadway musical), *1:* 126, 128, 129

Chicago Hope, 1: 146

Chicago magazine, *3:* 587

Chicago (movie), *1:* 176

Chicano literature, *4:* 727–34

Chicken, House, The (England), *2:* 231

Chief creative officers, *1:* 15, 19

Chief executive officers, *1:* 15, 52, 144; *3:* 435
    of eBay, Inc., *4:* 799–805
    of Hewlett-Packard, *2:* 221, 224–27
    of Time Warner, *3:* 561, 566–68
    of Yahoo!, *4:* 681

Chief operating officers, *4:* 682

Child labor, *3:* 464

Children
    human rights for, in Iran, *1:* 161–68

"Children of the Red King" series (Nimmo), *3:* 510

Children's literature, *2:* 229–35, 36–73; *3:* 491, 493–96, 505–11, 543, 545–49, 551, 554–58; *4:* 715, 717–19, 731–33

Childs, David, *2:* 419

"Child's Play" commercial, *1:* 57

Child's Reflections Cold Play, *1:* 111

Chimeres (Haitian security forces), *1:* 30

China, *3:* 574, 575; *4:* 800, 820, 821

China Beach, 4: 683

China Unicom, *4:* 826

Chinese Basketball Association, *4:* 822, 824, 825

Chloe house of design (Paris), *2:* 428, 431–32

Chopra, Deepak, *4:* 704

Christian music, *4:* 707, 708–9

Christmas Carol, A (play), *3:* 470

"Christmas Rappin'," *4:* 701

Chrysler-Plymouth Tournament of Champions (golf), *4:* 723

Chuck and Buck, 1: 38

Church, Charlotte, *2:* 306; *3:* 603

Cinderella, 1: 174

Cinderella Story, A, 1: 145, 149

Citrus Bowl, *1:* 64

City of Angels, 4: 778

Civil rights movement, *3:* 529, 624

Civil War, *2:* 222

CJ Nine Bridges Classic (golf), *4:* 809 (ill.)

Clarey, Christopher, *3:* 636

Clark, Dick, *4:* 677, 678

Clarkson, Patricia, *4:* 779

Clements, Kevin, *3:* 584

Clements, Mike, *1:* 12

Cleveland Cavaliers (basketball team), *2:* 350, 351, 353 (ill.), 354, 355

Climate changes
    embedded networked sensing and, *1:* 202

Climatology, *4:* 759–66

Clinton, Bill, *1:* 51, 53, 54; *3:* 501; *4:* 669

Clinton, George, *3:* 528, 529–30; *4:* 700

Clinton, Hillary, *4:* 704–5

Clippers (basketball team), *1:* 74

Cliques, *1:* 207

"Clocks" (Coldplay), *1:* 115

Closer, (Groban) *2:* 307–8

CNN, *3:* 564

Coalition government (India), *2:* 249

Cobain, Kurt, *2:* 385

Coca-Cola
    battle between Pepsi and, *3:* 515

Cocks, Jay, *2:* 359

Cohen, Adam, *3:* 566

"Cola wars," *3:* 515

Cold Mountain, 4: 796

Cold War, *3:* 626

Coldplay, *1:* **109–16,** 110 (ill.), 115 (ill.)

Colin Quinn: Back to Brooklyn, 4: 739

Collar, Matt, *2:* 390

Collins, David, *3:* 590, 591

Color of Money, The, 4: 739

Colorists (comic books), *3:* 445

Columbia Records, *2:* 217, 404

Columbia space shuttle, *4:* 649

Columbus, Chris, *3:* 600, 601, 603

Columbus, Christopher, *1:* 25

Combs, Sean P. Diddy, *2:* 217; *4:* 705

Comcast, *3:* 610

Come Away With Me, 2: 383, 387

Comedians, *1:* 131–37; *4:* 737–43

Johnson, Dwayne (The Rock), *2: 375–82,* 375
  (ill.), 381 (ill.)
    Rock Says, The, 2: 379–80
Johnson, Jack, *1:* 10
Johnson & Johnson, *3:* 514
Johnson, Lyndon, *1:* 57
Johnson, Peter, *4:* 657
Johnson, Philip, *2:* 264; *3:* 456
Johnson, Robert, *4:* 793
Johnson, Rocky, *2:* 376
Johnson Family Vacation, 2: 403
"Jokers through History" (Gaiman), *2:* 239
Jones, James Earl, *1:* 10
Jones, Norah, *2:* **383–91,** 383 (ill.), 388 (ill.), 406
Jones, Sue, *2:* 384
Jonze, Spike, *1:* 119
Joplin, Janis, *4:* 709
Jordan, Gregor, *1:* 50
Jordan, Michael, *2:* 349, 354, 355
Josh Groban in Concert, 2: 307
Journeys with George, 3: 574
Joyce, Dru II, *2:* 350
Joyce, Dru III, *2:* 352
Juan Carlos (king of Spain), *4:* 834, 834 (ill.)
Judd, Ashley, *2:* 333
Judging Amy, 4: 755
Julius (Johnson), *2:* 370
Junior, 4: 667
Jurassic Park, 3: 607
"Just Let Me Cry," *4:* 709
Just So Stories (Kipling), *2:* 231
Justified, 4: 767, 771
Justin Timberlake Foundation, *4:* 769
Juvenile Diabetes, *4:* 749

Ⓚ

Kael, Pauline, *3:* 463
Kallio, Sandra, *1:* 129
Kamen, Dean, *2:* **393–400,** 393 (ill.), 397 (ill.)
Kandasamy, Deepa, *2:* 300
Kangaroo Jack, 1: 9, 11, 12
Kasem, Casey, *4:* 677
Kate & Leopold, 2: 333
Kate McShane, 4: 738

Kattakayam, Jiby, *4:* 656
Katzenberg, Jeffrey, *1:* 177
kawaii concept (Japanese term for cuteness), *3:* 478
Keaton, Diane, *1:* 105 (ill.)
Keeling, Dan, *1:* 112, 113
Keeve, Douglas, *3:* 454
Kelley, David E., *2:* 305, 306
Kennedy, John F., *4:* 668
Kerry, John, *1:* 53, 57; *3:* 577; *4:* 704
Kessler, Ted, *2:* 218
Keys, Alicia, *2:* 406
Keyworth, George, *2:* 226
KFC, *3:* 516
Khatami, Mohammad, *1:* 165
Khomeini, Ayatollah Ruhollah Masawi, *1:* 162, 163, 164–65; *2:* 324
Khufu (Egyptian pharaoh), *2:* 295
Kidman, Nicole, *4:* 796
Kidney dialysis machines, *2:* 396
Kids, Fred, *1:* 18
Kids with a Cause, *1:* 150
Kightlinger, Laura, *1:* 40
"Killing Time," *2:* 404
Kilpatrick, Kwame, *4:* 703 (ill.)
Kim Possible, 1: 176
Kincheloe, Iven C., *4:* 649
Kindergarten Cop, 4: 667
Kindred, Dave, *1:* 66
King Kong, 1: 40
King Kong (1933 movie), *2:* 340, 346
Kingdom Come, 1: 11
Kingdom of Heaven, 1: 49
King's Ransom, 1: 11, 13
Kipling, Rudyard
    Just So Stories, 2: 231
Kirby, Jack, *2:* 331
Kirkpatrick, Christopher, *4:* 769, 770, 771
Kite Fighters, The (Park), *3:* 556
Kite fighting (Korea), *3:* 553, 556
Klein, Calvin, *3:* 453
Kloves, Steve, *3:* 600
Knight, Phil, *3:* 464
Knopf Publishers, *3:* 548
Knowles, Beyoncé, *1:* 189; *2:* **401–7,** 401 (ill.), 405 (ill.)
Knowles, Mathew, *2:* 402, 403, 404, 405
Knowles, Solange, *2:* 402, 403